*South
African
Tradition*

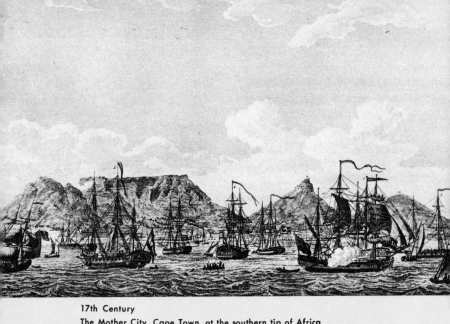

17th Century
The Mother City, Cape Town, at the southern tip of Africa
20th Century

SOUTH AFRICAN TRADITION

A brief survey
of the arts and cultures of
the diverse peoples
of South Africa

THIRD EDITION (1974)

The South African Department of Information
wishes to thank the following persons
and institutions for their contributions
to this book:

Prof. A. P. Grové
Prof. D. Ziervogel
Prof. Heather Martienssen
Dr. Barrie Bierman
Dr. Hugh Tracey
Mr. Ulrich Stark
Mr. Con Lamprecht
Prof. Leon Hugo
South African Broadcasting Corporation
Department of Sport and Recreation
Mr. Richard Daneel
Mrs. Frieda Harmsen

Photographs by kind permission:

Provincial Councils for the
Performing Arts
     CAPAB
     NAPAC
     PACOFS
     PACT
South African Tourist Corporation
South African Broadcasting Corporation
City Council of Pretoria
Johannesburg Civic Theatre
Department of Information

CONTENTS

INTRODUCTION   7

1. LITERATURE   9
    Afrikaans   10
    English   17
    Bantu   22

2. THE FINE ARTS   31

3. HANDICRAFTS   49
    Pottery   50
    Jewelry   52
    Tapestry   54
    Mosaic   56
    Batik   56
    Bantu Handicrafts   57

4. THE PERFORMING ARTS   61

5. MUSIC   69

6. IN LIGHTER VEIN   79
    Boeremusiek   79
    Folk Dancing   82
    Bantu Music   87

7. RADIO SOUTH AFRICA   97

8. MOTION PICTURE INDUSTRY   111

9. ARCHITECTURE   121

10. SPORTS AND RECREATION   132

REFERENCE LIST   142

The University of Cape Town, the oldest seat of learning in South Africa.

INTRODUCTION

South Africa, wrote Sarah Gertrude Millin, is not a country of lesser things. "There is no spring. There is no autumn. A dust-storm blows and brings the rain, and it is winter. A dust-storm blows and brings the rain, and it is summer. No seasonal vaguenesses. No stepping-stones. Summer. Winter . . ."

South African art is not a mirror of lesser things. It is not a mirror at all. It is part of life itself as lived by many and varied peoples in a multi-national land. And it is rarely given to vagueness because the land is South Africa. A dust-storm. Summer. Winter . . .

Sport in South Africa is not merely recreation. It is part of life and practised with passion. There is a victor and a vanquished . . . and somehow an aftermath of despondency should the battle end in a draw. In South Africa there is no room for vagueness. Summer. Winter . . .

There are those who seriously subscribe to a thesis which equates the flying pass in football to the pas de deux in ballet. We are not among those. Inclusion of sport in this little volume merely rounds out a theme which feeds on the outdoors and on all the features that are the face of South Africa. And it is part of a tradition . . .

hef haar gesig op en haar mond, oop en trillend, is naby
. „Lasarus slaap nie, hy is dood," sê sy en sluit haar oë.
em is sag en stukkend. „Wanneer kom Hy nog hier aan
voet moet loop? Dit sal amper twee dae duur . . ."
Hy nie 'n dogtertjie opgewek wat dood was nie?"
was anders met Jaïrus se dogtertjie," sê. „Sy was
ood, toe was Hy daar. Maar hier . . . Lasarus is al
od."

s stryk met sy hand die hare uit haar gesig weg, druk
en hom vas en daar is geen skeiding tussen hulle nie,
lle mekaar al baie jare ken. „Maria," sê hy, „ek dink
lat Lasarus dood is . . ."
Hoe kan Hy weet?"

...LITERATURE

want to go to Africa let me know." Passages were
to get and so he'd taken advantage of Simpson's
said, "Of course it's the wrong time of year there
as hell." And he'd said, "I don't care, I love the
"But why L.M.?" Simpson had said. "Why n
Town or Durban? If you like it hot you'd like
It's lovely, up on the Berea. Nice people too,
spectable and Rotary lot. Or go to Jo'burg if yc
not so respectable. Jo'burg's like a little New Yc
to drink, a lot of pretty women, race courses, gc
night clubs — the works in fact."

Imali yami O, imali yami, yek' imali yami.
Ngamshintsha upondo, ngamenza osheleni,
Ngaqond' eThwathwa, ngaphuza kancane.
Tshelani u6a6a O, tshelani umama,
Ngasuk' ekhaya nginesimilo.
Ngafika eGoli ngadliwa izindunduma.
Akenithule zingane zawo6a6a,
Nginitshele'inda6a zokuham6a.
Ngasuk' ekhaya ngiqond' omsebenzi,
Nagafika eGoli ngadliwa ezindunduma.
Ngangimthanda udali umaGumede,
l..du themba lami.

April 6, 1652. Jan van Riebeeck lands at the Cape of Good Hope bringing with him the Dutch language.

AFRIKAANS
youngest of the Germanic languages

It is impossible to fix the precise date of birth of Afrikaans. We do know, however, that when Jan van Riebeeck and his men arrived at the Cape in 1652 they spoke Dutch. In the process of colonization the language of these colonists gradually altered to such an extent that, from about 1750, it was regarded as a separate language, Afrikaans, the youngest of the Germanic languages. There were various reasons for this development. Apart from a gradual change in syntax and morphology, new words were borrowed, in the course of time, from indigenous languages and later from the French, German and English immigrants. Afrikaans thus acquired an identity of its own, quite distinct from Dutch, while retaining its Germanic character.

Afrikaans, however, was not given full recognition during these early years. It was the vernacular, while Dutch remained the official language of the church, the school and the state. This strained situation was to persist right up to the 'twenties of this century.

With the British occupation of the Cape (1795) and the rapidly growing influence of English, Afrikaans for obvious reasons, would seem to have had a better chance of survival than Dutch. Its progress was, however, hampered in that it had no tradition as a written language. It was against this background that the G.R.A. *(Genootskap van Regte Afrikaners* — the Association of True Afrikaners) was founded at Paarl in 1875. This group of enthusiasts strove, purposefully, often in the face of violent criticism, to gain acceptance of Afrikaans as a written language. After the Anglo-Boer War (1899-1902) came the rise of the Second Language Movement, which, under new leadership, operated throughout the country and immediately produced work of significance. Afrikaans now gradually gained the upper hand over Dutch and achieved recognition as a school language (1914), a language of the church (1916-1919), and in 1925, it replaced Dutch as one of the two official languages together with English.

This recognition led to a period of inspired cultural activity which was reflected in the poetic outburst of the 1930's; the Afrikaans translation of the Bible and the Psalm Book took place in 1933 and 1934 respectively.

Afrikaans is a virile and growing language. Originally a language of the 'veld' and the 'soil', it has adapted itself to all the needs of a modern society. It is a language not only of the farmer, but also of the factory worker, the scholar and the poet. Today Afrikaans is taught in every school and university in South Africa, and in most of these institutions

S. V. Petersen, one of the most influential Coloured poets. Petersen has produced some of the best poetry in the Afrikaans language.

Nicholaas Petrus van Wyk Louw — foremost of the Afrikaans poets. Louw spent some time as professor in Afrikaans language and literature at the University of the Netherlands, Amsterdam.

it is the medium of instruction. Many foreign universities offer courses in Afrikaans and at the University of Amsterdam a chair of Afrikaans Language and Literature has been founded.

Before 1900 only a few Afrikaans literary works of any significance were produced. The Afrikaans poetic tradition really came into being at the beginning of this century with the poetry of J. D. du Toit (Totius), C. L. Leipoldt, Jan Celliers and Eugene Marais, who each in their own way tried to give meaning to the traumatic experience of the Anglo-Boer War.

The 1920's brought new problems in politics, economics and religion and these were reflected to a certain extent in the works of Toon van den Heever and his generation. But the full flowering of Afrikaans poetry was witnessed only in

New Dictionary for a new language.

the 1930's when poets such as N. P. van Wyk Louw (1906-1970), Uys Krige (born 1910) and Elizabeth Eybers (born 1916) started to dominate the literary scene. A more conscious craftsmanship became immediately noticeable, as well as a finer feeling for the exact word and a desire to produce something beautiful and lasting. Afrikaans poetry acquired a professional character.

In the works of each of these poets we can see a definite development from the lyrical to more objective expression. This is especially true of van Wyk Louw, the pacemaker of his generation. From the lyrical song he moved via the epic poem, the modern balled and the dramatic monologue, to the poetic drama, e.g. *Germanicus.* One of the main stages of this development was marked by the modern epic *Raka,* in which is depicted the downfall of a people who unthinkably laid themselves open to the sinister influence of the earth-bound being *Raka.* It is no simple allegory; within the framework of this tragic story the conflict between the two major figures, Raka, and the spiritual leader, Koki, acquires great symbolic

Elisabeth Eybers — poet.   André Brink — novelist.

significance. It becomes the struggle between order and chaos,
the persuasive, rational *word* opposed to the blind unthinking
act, the spirit opposed to brute corporality, civilization against
nature. This great poem has been translated into English
and German.

The poetry of the 'forties was characterized by a strong
sense of actuality. This was particularly noticeable in the
work of D. J. Opperman (born 1914). The realities of the
South African situation, the country and its peoples, its
animals and plants, its history, political tensions and involved
racial problems, these were the things that caught his eye.
He does not merely depict reality however. He is the 'ex-
plorer' and also the 'scribe', and the more he exposes
himself to the infinite complexity of the universe, the more
he feels himself impelled to discover it in an underlying
significance, freeing "the angel from the stone". Opperman
had the poetic equipment for doing this. With his meta-
phorical gifts, his ability through historical and biblical
allusions to strike bridges across time and space, he often

14

A gathering of poets, 1966. Left to right: S. J. Pretorius, E. van Heerden, D. J. Opperman and the late N. P. van Wyk Louw.

succeeded in giving to a basic theme a universal meaning.

In the 1950's van Wyk Louw, Elizabeth Eybers and Opperman produced some of their most mature work. Even in the 'sixties they were the leading figures in Afrikaans literature, while younger voices began to ring out clearly beside theirs; those of Olga Kirsch, P. Philander, Adam Small, Peter Blum, Ina Rousseau and Breyten Breytenbach. It can be noted that non-Afrikaners are availing themselves more and more of Afrikaans as a creative language. Olga Kirsch is Jewish, Philander and Small are Coloured, while Blum, who was born in Trieste and came to South Africa as a boy, has adopted Afrikaans as his home language.

In this short survey, Afrikaans poetry has been emphasized and justly so. Authors like C. M. van den Heever, J. van Bruggen, J. van Melle and A. A. Pienaar have produced a number of fine novels and have, in the process, explored the local scene in numerous directions. In recent years younger writers (F.A. Venter, Henriette Grové, Etienne Leroux,

15

Ettiènne Leroux.

André Brink, Jan Rabie, Chris Barnard and Karl Schoeman) explored new avenues in the drama, novel and short story writing and have experimented with various modern techniques. A number of their works have been translated into English, Dutch and German, e.g. *The Ambassador* (Brink) and *Seven Days at the Silbersteins* (Leroux). But it is in the field of poetry that Afrikaans has reached its highest attainment. In the course of sixty years, it has produced poetry that is recognized by critics, wherever Afrikaans is understood, as a valuable contribution to the literature of our age.

SOUTH AFRICA'S ENGLISH LITERATURE

— old language, new image

The English language and, by extension, English literature, was permanently established in southern Africa at the start of the second British Occupation of the Cape in 1806. Records show that the new administration included several versifiers — men who, like their compatriots in other distant places, composed odes, in honor of the King's birthday or mused in rhyming couplets on the wonders of the new Colony.

Such poetry had no literary worth, but mere historic interest, (reflecting a 'colonial' sensibility) determinedly British in an environment not only alien but also fortuitous.

Colonialism dominated poetry for over a century. In the early years only one man of talent, *Thomas Pringle,* seriously tried to portray the Africa he had discovered. Pringle was a gifted man, and *S. T. Coleridge* praised his work highly; but today even his best poem *"Afar in the Desert"* jars with the discord between subject and idiom. Late in the nineteenth century, *W. C. Scully* went further than anyone had hitherto gone in creating a suitable idiom, but it was *Francis Carey Slater* who, from the turn of the century onward, developed the first authentic 'voice'. Slater was a less gifted exponent of an indigenous poetic idiom, but a determined champion of it; he may fairly be called the father of South African English poetry, and a work such as *"Drought"* (1929) was no mean achievement.

FAR LEFT: Sarah Gertrude Millin. LEFT: The young Olive Schreiner at the time of writing "The Story of an African Farm".

A young contemporary, *Roy Campbell,* represents the apex of the growth away from 'colonialism'. He burst upon the literary scene in the nineteen-twenties, and, temperamentally a radical, he soon became the most unpopular genius the country had produced. In such poems as *"The Zebras", "The Flaming Terrapin",* and the *"Wayzgoose"* we find a most colorful and vital declaration of natural genius welded to the country of its origin.

Campbell's international reputation tended to obscure those of lesser but nonetheless considerable men and women. Consider the works of his contemporary, *William Plomer,* whose *"The Scorpion",* among other scarcely less remarkable poems, is a little masterpiece: and in the nineteen-thirties and 'forties writers such as *Mary Morison Webster, R. N. Currey,* and *Rico Titelstad* established the idiom in reflective, personal pieces.

Since the war, and with the rapid growth of industrial cities, English poetry has become more urban in outlook, more cosmopolitan. This trend has brought it closer to prevailing international poetic modes; at the same time its roots in the South African soil have gone deeper. *Guy Butler* and *Anthony Delius* among the older generation, *Sydney Clouts* and *Douglas Livingstone* among the younger, have produced works of distinction.

A feature of the contemporary scene is the appearance of a number of avant-garde poetry magazines. The quality is uneven and none has yet brought Roy Campbell's successor to light, but several committed new voices, notably that of *Wopko Jensma,* show a healthy interest in the medium.

Prose writing before 1880 was like poetry, heavily 'colonial'. Travel books and descriptive 'novels' were written for an almost exclusively European market. Then in 1883 *The Story of an African Farm* was published in London. It startled the literary world, as much by its vivid evocation of the vast Karoo as by the depth of insight of its young author, *Olive Schreiner.* General J. C. Smuts was echoing

ABOVE: Nadine Gordimer
TOP RIGHT: Roy Campbell
RIGHT: William Plomer

the opinion of generations of South Africans when he spoke of the intensity of the genius of this remarkable woman. She was a flame which burned too fiercely . . . and the fact is that Olive Schreiner was not again able to scale the heights of *An African Farm*. Among her own writings as well as those of her contemporaries this novel had a solitary splendor.

The discovery of diamonds and gold, the *Anglo-Boer War* and the movement to Union gave some impetus to prose fiction — generally as an inferior, anecdotal kind. Slight exceptions were Scully's novels, Douglas Blackburn's *Prinsloo of Prinsloodorp* (1899) and Richard Dehan's *The Dop*

19

Doctor (1910) a best seller about the siege of Mafeking. The only enduring classic of this period was Percy Fitzpatrick's dog story, *Jock of the Bushveld* (1907).

It was another woman, *Pauline Smith,* who re-discovered the rich vein that Olive Schreiner had struck. Her book, *The Beadle* (1926), is a moving and sensitive account of life in the Little Karoo. And it was yet a third woman, *Sarah Gertrude Millin,* who finally and firmly established the South African English novel as a distinctive type. In her long and distinguished career, in such books as *The Coming of the Lord* (1928) and *What Hath a Man?* Mrs. Millin secured a pre-eminent position for herself.

Other novelists before and after the 1939-45 war produced a considerable body of work, but the tendency is to associate the author with one or two titles only. *Turbott Wolfe* (1925) by *Plomer* was regarded by Campbell as one of the 'richest and most imaginative prose works that has come out of Africa'. *In a Province* (1934) Laurens van der Post established a reputation which a long and productive career has maintained. *Cry, the Beloved Country* (1948) by Alan Paton was internationally acclaimed; (and more recently) *Episode* (1956) by Harry Bloom and *A Dance in the Sun* (1956) by Dan Jacobson show that a virile future is assured for the novel.

The short story has been well served. Pauline Smith's *The Little Karoo* (1925), deservedly a minor classic, has had its measure of recognition. One cannot say the same of H. C. Bosman's collection *Mafeking Road* (1947), the humorous ironies of which have been neglected. In the 1970's, through Jack Cope, Dan Jacobson, and especially *Nadine Gordimer* — one of the most incisively intelligent writers in English today — the South African short story reaches an international audience.

Athol Fugard is the only dramatist of note. *The Blood Knot, People are Living There* and *Boesman and Lena* are plays that denote a significant talent.

Non-fiction writing ranges from Burchell's *Travels in Southern Africa* in the nineteenth century (and van der Post's *Venture into the Interior* in this century) to Olive Schreiner's polemics on behalf of women's rights, to any number of studies of the indigenous peoples of southern Africa, J. C. Smith's philosophical treatise, *Holism and Evolution,* several biographies, autobiographies and histories.

Deneys Reitz's *Commando* and Rayne Kruger's *Goodbye Dolly Gray* probably give the best 'popular' accounts of the *Anglo-Boer War*. Sarah Gertrude Millin's *Smuts* and Alan Paton's *Hofmeyer* are outstanding biographies of two controversial figures.

The growth of English literature over the past ninety years has been inextricably linked with a growth of awareness of the problems facing South Africa. Nearly all the writers mentioned above have been involved in the issues of the day, the still unresolved one, that of race relations, overriding all others. The general tendency has been liberal, proof (if that were needed) that the old 'colonialism', as exemplified in English literature, has infused the indigenous culture with the best of a centuries-old tradition.

21

A typical Karoo scene

LEFT: Dr. E. S. Moloto, Tswana writer, who obtained his doctorate on a thesis: "The Growth and Tendencies of Tswana Poetry".

ABOVE: D. B. Ntuli, Zulu novelist and poet.

BANTU LITERATURE

— traditional folklore evolves into modern writing

Although the South African Bantu population is distinctly divided into eight national and language entities of which seven languages are used in writing, a similarity in literature and language exists between them comparable perhaps to that of the Germanic, Slavic or the Romance peoples of Europe.

The South African Bantu have only in the last 50-60 years emerged from literary isolation. Their contact with the White element over more than two centuries has influenced their literary views. In the old society they produced their traditional lore to which the term oral or traditional "literature" (though it was not written) is applied. These traditional literatures survived orally; they were retold from generation to generation and adapted to changing times, so that today traditional lore has an old and a new stratum. Stories with traditional themes exist side by side with those having modern themes.

The traditional lore of the Bantu consisted mainly of a variety of narratives. There was the folktale told for the sake of amusement which was mainly the prerogative of the old women. Folktales were told at night lest one grew horns on the head, undoubtedly an ingenious way of keeping children occupied by more serious business than mere story-telling. There were the ogres, deceitful rogues who by some ruse got their victims in a bag. But evil could not be overcome and soon the victims were rescued by playing up to the vanity of the ogre.

These were fables in which humans were presented in the guise of animals. For the most part all stories ended in a moral. Proverbs played an important role in educating the youth. In these distilled words of wisdom the philosophy of the ancients was expressed. The fables reflected the ancestor's life and thoughts. They embodied the basic traditional values based on the experiences of past generations. In them the unwritten laws were laid down.

On the other hand riddles presented the humorous and the lighter side of tradition. As a teaching medium they contained a grain of truth which was derived from keen observation of the world around them.

Of all the oral literary output the praise-poems, variously known as *isibongo, dithoko, maboko, direto,* were the highest attainment in literary sophistication. They dealt with boys attending initiation, with warriors and kings and finally with birds and cattle. The most accomplished praise-poems were those dealing with kings. A reciter of praise-poems jumped about brandishing his spear while reciting in a high-pitched voice the brave deeds of a warrior king. He was able to criticize the ruler in the name of his people, but in the style of the praise-poet. His language was poetic and rhythmic, alluding to deeds and incidents in the life of the king so lauded.

A large number of praise-poems in the various languages have been collected into volumes. Prof. Nyembezi's annotated collection of the praises of the Zulu Kings *(Izibongo Zamakhosi)* is one of the most outstanding collections. Traditional lore has not lost its flavor. It is still practised.

The late B. Wallet Vilakazi, a writer of historical romances but better known as a poet, wrote a thesis on Zulu poetry which he condensed into an article *The Conception and Development of Poetry in Zulu,* 1938. In 1967 Dr. S. M. Guma wrote *The Form, Content and Technique of Traditional Literature in Southern Sotho* in which he dealt with the whole range of indigenous literature in Southern Sotho, a work worth reading to obtain a background to the genres of indigenous lore. E. S. Moloto's thesis on *The Growth and Tendencies of Tswana Poetry* analyzes the traditional poetry, showing not only the formal patterns of the poetry but also the role of *inter alia,* the metaphor and the subtlety of imagery. This is followed by a critical appreciation of modern poetry in Tswana.

These were the beginnings of a critical appreciation of the literary production in the Bantu languages by Bantu scholars themselves.

The Whites brought knowledge of writing to the Bantu. They also became acquainted with Western literature. It was thus inevitable that there should be some interchange of form and content. They consequently began to write their own languages in European style. That history played its part is

University of the North library.

understandable, for the greatness of the past lingered in the thoughts of a generation which saw or heard at first hand of the decline of the old empires and their rulers. Thomas Mofolo, perhaps the greatest of the classical writers, produced his *Tjhaka,* a historical romance in which the Zulu tyrant Shaka is exposed in a fictitious setting of witchdoctors and ancestral manifestations such as is found in the *Great Snake,* a work of enormous impact and psychological insight. Vilakazi, while better known as a poet, also wrote historical novels, among his best perhaps one that gives a fine exposition of the Bhambatha Rebellion of 1906. On the whole Vilakazi is inclined to unnecessary detail. The Northern Sotho writer, Makgaleng, dramatized the *History of Matlebjane* exposing court intrigues. Khaketla, writing in Southern Sotho, depicted the great Moshweshwe as a man of peace and progress.

The social novel has of late begun to supersede history. Professor Nyembezi, one of the outstanding and most prolific

Zulu poet, M. T. Mazibuko.

Zulu writers, has shown a gift for portraying characters. This is in contrast to the majority of Bantu authors who on the whole are more given to descriptive writing and, to some extent, moralizing. Nyembezi deals with the errant and recalcitrant boy who becomes a murderer, or the learned lawyer who is a rogue. Some Bantu novelists have also turned to writing of the impact of 20th century civilization on the

26

Bantu. In urbanization they seem to find only evil. Hence the so-called *makgoweng* (going to the Whites) motif in which the urban youngsters go to the great cities to find work but fall into evil ways. The authors themselves are still feeling their way about, much like the characters they depict. The works of J. J. R. Jolobe the eminent Xhosa author, range from novels to essays and poetry. Unlike the Xhosa bard Mqhayi who was indeed a writer for the people, Jolobe is more sophisticated, using a style perhaps more in the taste of the Westernized Bantu.

Love had until recently little part in Bantu literature. Older generation authors tackled the clash between the old customs and modern individualism, especially in the choice of a wife. Where in traditional society a wife was chosen by the parents, the urban youth could no longer abide by parental decision. It was, however, not love which was depicted by simply a desire to choose one's own mate without prescription by others.

A theme which seems to have crept into Bantu literature, especially Sotho writing, is the clash between Christianity and traditional ancestral worship. Novelists show the modern Bantu groping about to find a way in which to reconcile the ancestral spirits and the Christian God. In Matlala's *Kgokong-e-ntsho* (a concoction of certain parts of the human body to bring about rain) the main character turns to the Christian God rather than to the ancestral spirits to ensure the success of his heathen mission to kill a young boy in order to obtain the necessary ingredients for his medicine.

The Bantu author is in many respects entangled in tradition and custom on the one hand, and Western values on the other. He depicts his own people, showing them in a state of transition — the new cannot simply supersede the old, there must be evolutionary development. If in this process the author himself is not sure of his own attitude towards a problem he mainly describes and portrays but does not resolve the problem.

The poet is in a similar plight. He has, on the one hand, the traditional praise-poem which is communally and personally directed; on the other hand there is Western individualism. Many poets, such as the Sotho Mmamogobo, endeavor to be individualistic but cannot entirely break with the praise-poem. This individualism is the main characteristic of modern Bantu poetry, not only in content but in form as well. The free rhythm of the praise-poem must make room for the Western meter and other formal devices such as rhyme. Vilakazi, the Zulu poet, was first to break with the praise-poem in trying to grapple with newfound individualism and lyricism. Modern Sotho poets like Lesoro and Machaka are exponents of this poetry. The Xhosa Jolobe has moved furthest away from the traditional.

Modern Bantu prose literature, including drama, is slowly outgrowing the stage when the main aim was to moralize, Bantu authors are gradually tackling the problems of their times, mainly the clash between what is generally referred to as the old and the new. The themes run on a broad plane, from the evils of urban life to the individualism of the emerging Black man and his general state of transition. As medium the social novel is best suited to this tendency. Social changes, shown as synonymous with social decline, form the basic theme. Although many of these works reflect life in the cities no author has as yet escaped completely from his rural background, because of the strong link between urban and rural life. Hence the tendency in the prose literature of today to portray tradition and problems resulting from contact with new cultures; the most convincing poetry is that with strong undertones of the tradition.

Most recent publications in Bantu literature show signs of a change in thought and themes. Individualism is strongly making itself felt in poetry particularly. The modern poet wrestles with the problem of life and death as it affects himself. The link with the community of which he is a part is very weak and traditional values play almost no part.

Although this cannot always be said of Bantu prose literature, there are indications of new themes set against a view of life of which Christianity is an accepted part. The tendency to moralize is diminishing, morality being subtly introduced by setting it against the criterion of Christian principles, and with character portrayal becoming more balanced. Love as a topic is becoming increasingly popular and it is depicted on its own merit without the intervention of tribal custom. Even topics verging on those found in detective stories are beginning to appear. The short story is also becoming a popular genre, and the authors seem to be familiar with the ingredients that make a good short story. Unfortunately these signs of a change have not yet permeated into Bantu drama literature.

This new look in Bantu literature is found especially in the works of younger writers such as O. K. Matsepe, a novelist and poet in Northern Sotho and I. Maditsi, a poet in the same language. D. D. Ntuli is a Zulu poet, short story writer and novelist who stands out as an exponent of the new approach to literature. Others are J. Gumbi, a novelist, and T. M. Mazibuko, a promising poet.

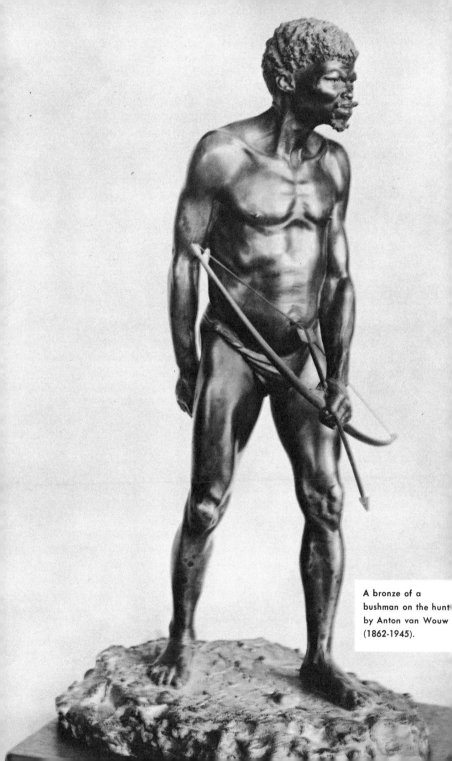

A bronze of a bushman on the hunt by Anton van Wouw (1862-1945).

Earliest existing painting of ships in Table Bay by van Rhijn, 1720.

THE FINE ARTS

In the art of the rocks South Africa has something rare and great. All the evidence points to the fact that the Bushmen were the authors of most, if not all, of the prehistoric art of South Africa. They are a short-statured people and were among the first inhabitants of what is today the Republic of South Africa. They have consistently refused to be 'civilized' and a remaining few are still living their Stone Age lives in the seclusion of the Kalahari desert.

There are more than 2,000 recorded sites with prehistoric art in South Africa, some as fine as any in France and Spain.

The principal subject of the art was animals hunted by the Bushmen, but snakes, birds and even insects are shown. Human figures are also common, usually in action — dancing, hunting, or fighting — as are the strange creatures of Bushmen mythology: horned snakes, huge bogey animals, winged

Bushman rock painting.

Oil painting of the English settlers' landing, 1820 by Thomas Baines.

antelope and beings half-animal and half-human like the Cretan Minotaur. There are even paintings of domestic cattle and horses complete with tack and white riders proving that the artists were still active when the Bantu with their herds and the European pioneer on horseback penetrated the mountainous domain. Perhaps the best-known are in the

Marble frieze detail in the Voortrekker (Pioneer) Monument, Pretoria, depicting details of The Great Trek of 1838.

33

Drakensberg. The Natal Parks Board has preserved one of the more important shelters in the Giant's Castle reserve as a field museum.

The artists preferred to paint in the rock shelters formed by nature in the sandstone and granite of the mountains which provided them with their homes. On the exposed rocks on the koppies, where the paint could not last long, they chose to engrave, cutting away the dark patinated surface of the ironstone to expose the lighter color beneath, thus producing a colored picture without the use of paint.

When the Europeans came to the country in the seventeenth century, they were unaware of the art galleries in the rock shelters, and would probably not have been interested anyway. The settlers at the Cape eventually felt the need of prestigious homes, suitably decorated with carved doors, fanlights and sculpture in the tradition of their forefathers in Europe. Sites, climate and the specialized needs of the settlers however, brought forth an architecture that was quite distinct from its European prototypes, and is known today as the Cape-Dutch style.

Glowing yellow-wood doors, window frames and shutters, wide stoeps shaded by grape-bearing pergolas, sweeping curvilinear gables and warm thatched roofs, give an aristocratic dignity to the buildings. Set within green vineyards against the blue Cape mountains they are redolent of the graceful living we now nostalgically believe to have flourished in the eighteenth-century Cape.

Louis Thibault (1750-1815) was an architect responsible for many fine eighteenth-century buildings in Cape Town, including the Government Buildings, and Anton Anreith (1754-1822), was a sculptor whose accomplished work on many major buildings, in and near Cape Town can easily be distinguished from that by lesser craftsmen.

It was not until the middle of the nineteenth century before one could speak of any significant painting in the European tradition belonging to South Africa. Today the work by people such as Thomas Bowler (1813-1869), Thomas Baines (1820-1875), George Angas (1822-1886) and Frederick I'ons (1802-1887) — the names of only four of the better painters — is regarded with keen interest by Africana scholars.

They produced a quaint recording of the country, shipping, animals, human inhabitants, customs and adventures seen and experienced by pioneers. They were often made to send 'home' to England so that the people there might see what the 'Barbaric South' was like. Many of these pictures were engraved for publication in the 'London Illustrated News'. Their work has great documentary value, and is therefore usually found in historical and cultural museums rather than in art galleries.

Like poetry, western art with aesthetic value did not emerge in South Africa before the beginning of the twentieth century. At first it was Impressionistic in style. The Dutch immigrants, Pieter Wenning (1872-1922) and Frans Oerder (1867-1944) painted in the dark, somber style of the Hague School and the Amsterdam Impressionists. They favored gray skies and rainy days when they painted landscapes with green trees and peaceful cows. In time they were both lured, in spite of temperament and background, to attempt to depict South Africa's bright light and arid color.

These two men did not only depict the landscape in paintings and graphic work, but produced still lifes and portraits too. The academic Oerder especially was partial to meticulous portraiture and very popular, but uninspired flower-pieces.

A friend and compatriot of the two painters was the sculptor Anton van Wouw (1862-1945), who was affectionately recognized as the artist of the Transvaal Boere. Van Wouw was a realist to such an extent that he is sometimes dismissed as nothing more than a copyist. This criticism is unfair because from time to time Van Wouw could create sensitively in both monumental works (his monument to the

Voortrekker women in Bloemfontein is particularly successful) and small drawing room pieces.

The small works often depict the Afrikaner soldier, Voortrekker girls and Africans — working in the mines, drinking beer, smoking dagga, hunting or standing in the judicial dock. He worked in bronze (and it was Van Wouw who brought the Italian bronze caster, Vignali, to South Africa) but there is one marble carving of a seated Boer, executed while Van Wouw was in Italy, attributed to him.

Although Wenning lived many years in the Transvaal, the Cape was his favorite painting terrain, and it was in the peninsula that his influence was remarkably strong. One could even speak of a "Wenning School". Significant painters belong to the "group", the most important being perhaps Nita Spilhaus (1878-1967) and Gregoire Boonzaier (b. 1909). Not only is Gregoire important as a painter, but also as an ambassador for art. He did much to bring art to the rural districts with his travelling exhibitions and lectures.

Two contemporaries of Wenning, Hugo Naudé (1869-1941) and Strat Caldecott (1886-1929) followed the sunny and spontaneous French Impressionist style. Naudé was known in Worcester, the little Cape village where he lived, as 'the artist', and he has gone down in history as the first born South African to have followed that calling professionally.

Pieter Wenning showed an affinity for the surroundings of the Cape as in this "View from the Malay Quarter".

Hendrik Pierneef, deeply in love with the majestic beauty of the South African bushveld, recreated that beauty in scenes like "Entabeni" below.

Strat Caldecott's appealing pictures are distinctive, because they betray the artist's awareness of the South African white light so clearly.

Subsequently other artists also attempted to portray the harsh luminosity of our landscape, but the first probably to succeed entirely, was Jacob Hendrik Pierneef (1886-1957). He was also one of the first to break away from the gentle descriptive depictions of the landscape. He gave it a formal organization, submitted it, under the influence of the Dutch Cubist Konijnenburg, to a cerebral pattern that was evocative of the expansive, arid sun-bleached land.

ABOVE: Irma Stern
(1894-1966).

RIGHT:
Black sculptor
Sydney Kumalo,
created
"The Dancers".

LEFT: "Girl
with a recorder"
— painted by
Irma Stern in 1951.

While Pierneef emerged as the national favorite, several other artists during the period 1920-1930 were breaking away from academic realism and gentle Impressionism to introduce new and modern elements to our painting.

A family known as the Everard Group — consisting of Bertha Everard (1873- 1965), her sister E. L. M. King (1870-1962) and Bertha's daughters, Rosamund (1907-1945) and Ruth (b. 1904) all painted landscape in a bold, decorative way. Even Miss King's small watercolors betray a strength of purpose and design as powerful as her sister's large canvasses.

Shortly after the First World War, a more expressionistic style which had succeeded the Impressionists in France and

Germany, was introduced to South Africa by painters Irma Stern (1894-1966) and Maggie Laubser (1886-1972). Maggie saw the gentle pathos of the Cape fisherfolk, farm laborers, flowers and domestic animals, especially ducks and cats. Irma Stern saw the fierce pride of her fellow men — white, coloured and black. While Maggie Laubser's work is reserved and humble, Irma Stern's is emotional and turbulent. Both have a remarkable power that was first violently resisted by a startled public, but now venerated.

Wolf Kibel (1903-1938), an immigrant who came from Poland in 1929, was another Expressionist painter who had a considerable following in South Africa during his short career.

By the 1940's several of the older artists had established South African art on a professional level, and served to set the standard for the younger artists. The influential people — of whom many are still active today — are Moses Kottler (b. 1896), Coert Steynberg (b. 1906) and Lippy Lipschitz (b. 1903), all sculptors, and the painters Jean Welz (b. 1900), Cecil Higgs (b. 1906), Walter Battis (b. 1906) and Alexis Preller (b. 1911).

The dignified work of Moses Kottler is classical in its simplicity, throbbing with an inner emotion.

Lippy Lipschitz is perhaps the first South African sculptor to have produced intensely emotional work, and he did much to liberate and educate the staid South African public, where art appreciation is concerned, by confronting them with controversial works.

Coert Steynberg can be regarded as Van Wouw's successor. He is known primarily for his monumental sculpture glorifying South African heroes and ideologies, but I believe that his true personality in all its variations and moods is to be seen in his smaller works. One of the most recent works (1971) is an astonishing head cut from stone. It is distorted in its ruggedness, changing completely from every vantage

ABOVE: Black artist Azaria Mbatha depic "Scenes from the Bibl in this 1966 lino cut.

LEFT: Professor Walter Battis and one of his works.

point. It is compelling, vigorous, a triumphant statement of what an established sculptor can do.

Jean Welz and Cecil Higgs infuse their expressionistic work with a romantic aura thereby producing paintings that are both powerful and gentle. Welz frequently turns to the mountains for his subject, while Cecil Higgs is drawn to the sea. Welz is a painfully meticulous painter. His nudes are perhaps the finest in South African art, and never fail to enchant.

Maud Sumner (b. 1902) is often called the international artist because she spends half the year in London, half in Paris, and comes to South Africa from time to time to exhibit and paint. Her early work was purely, lyrically Impressionist (or Post-Impressionist), portraying landscapes and sometimes people in a gentle mood. Her latest work, usually depicting the desert of the Holy Land or South West Africa, can be said to be metaphysical through its lack of outline and hazy atmospheric color.

Walter Battis and Alexis Preller are regarded as two of the greatest and most influential living South African artists of the older generation.

Battiss is known as a teacher as well as an artist and writer. His paintings, drawings, graphics and photographs have been inspired by art manifestations in Europe and ancient folk art in Greece, Iran, Arabia and Turkey. For a while his painting and graphic work were strongly influenced by Bushmen art. He is always on the move, investigating, absorbing, and when he comes home we can see his experiences reflected in sublime or crazy pictures, and read about it in his lavishly illustrated and poetically written books.

Alexis Preller is a formidable artist whose enigmatic work stands somewhat aloof from other South African work as if preserved in a temple. Even when it hangs in a home it stands apart, rather like a religious icon. It can be said to represent the intangible and undefinable spirit of Africa.

Edoardo Villa (b. 1920), an Italian who came to South

Africa immediately after World War II, brought about a radical change in our sculpture. Soon he was to become the major sculptor of the younger artists. His most recent works are large massive hunks of bronze clearly derived from the human form, but rock-like in their immobility. Adults admire them for they recognize, perhaps, a technological tyrant that haunts our thinking. Children love them because they make the most wonderful playthings. Children and Villa sculpture go well together.

Cecil Skotnes (b. 1926) has an equally formidable imagery, but rather than forsee the technological man, Skotnes recreates man's archetype. This ostensibly pagan work has such profound humanity that involuntarily one may read religious content into it.

When South African art is seen as a whole it merges intrinsically as a landscape art, or perhaps one should say a rural art. Most of our artists who were born in the 'twenties' and 'thirties' have at some time or other produced 'abstract landscapes'. A few are prominent. Kenneth Bakker (b. 1926), Gunther van der Reis (b. 1927), Wim Blom (b. 1927) and Aileen Lipkin (b. 1933) have isolated the primeval elements of earth and sea. Their compositions depict the world in a state of incomplete creation. They are roughly textured, the heavy earth colors are often gritty, the shapes are rounded like ancient rocks, or amorphous, flowing like sluggish lava.

Two immigrants from Italy, Armando Baldinelli (b. 1908) and Guiseppe Cattaneo (b. 1929) were also bewitched by this enigma of an ancient dormant land. Baldinelli's powerful assemblages (often made from bleached, contorted tree stumps, rocks, pottery, glass and wrecks off the roads) and Cattaneo's sophisticated, pure paintings are perhaps among the most "African" of our modern landscapes.

Eric Laubscher (b. 1927) and Anna Vorster (b. 1928) superimpose dynamic lines on their compositions. Paul du Toit (b. 1922) and Lawrence Scully (b. 1922) are romantic

Alexis Preller captured the feeling of an unspoilt Africa in his gigantic mural "Discovery", completed in 1963.

painters, enveloping their forms in a diaphonous atmosphere evoking the sensation of misty vistas or rainy skies. George Boys (b. 1920) creates a brilliantly colored and glowing underwater fantasy world.

Colors in the paintings of Christo Coetzee (b. 1930) are flamboyant and dramatic, the surface is often encrusted, jewel-like, with coins and projecting paint of brilliant hue. Design occurs in two variations: open, liquid-floating forms which blossom into decorative rhythms and closed, single-image formations, invariably based upon the circle which spin toward the viewer like glowing astral orbs.

43

Gerard Sekoto, prominent Black painter and one of his works.

Wildlife is now a popular subject for South Africa artists, but the most significant artists of this genre are Gordon Vorster (b. 1925), Zakkie Eloff (b. 1925), Frits Krampe (1913-1966) and the young woodcutter, Raymond Andrews (b. 1948).

For a while Cecily Sash (b. 1925) painted birds, and can therefore be included in the wild life group. One of her best-known bird compositions is Seekoeivlei (1962), a large mosaic made for the cafeteria in the Transvaal Provincial Administration Building in Pretoria. A successor to this panel is the giant mosaic of butterflies (completed in 1970) that dominates the overseas departure hall of the Jan Smuts Airport near Johannesburg. Cecily Sash is an important artist who assiduously studies art movements, theories and methods, experiments with them in her own work and then conveys what she has learned to her students at the Witwatersrand University Art School.

Two of her most interesting pupils are Transvaal based Judith Mason (b. 1938) and Nils Burwitz (b. 1940). Judith Mason's themes are often religious, but far removed from the gentle imagery one may associate with religious painting. Her work is disturbing and intensely thought-provoking.

Nils Burwitz shocks his spectators out of their complacency equally forcibly. But whereas Judith uses traditional themes and forms to convey timeless ideas of mankind, Burwitz is sharply, hair-raisingly satirical.

LEFT: Red ivory wood statuette, "Supplication" an early work of Coert Steynberg.

RIGHT: Coert Steynberg as portrayed in oil by Irmin Henkel, 1965.

Other graduates from the Witwatersrand art school that are drawing favorable attention are Margaret McKean, Olivia Watson (b. 1944) Ulrich Louw (b. 1935) John Borchard (b. 1944) and Maurice Kahn (b. 1943). Margaret McKean's intellectually conceived and technically clean work is always enthusiastically received by the critics. Olivia Watson's work is tumultuous, always controversial and good enough to win repeated scholarships and commissions. One of her most recent works is a large mural in the Jan Smuts Airport. Louw, a school art master, first worked in the Pop idiom, now in a more surrealist-romantic vein. Borchard is a sculptor whose fiberglas bulls are both startling and amusing, and Kahn, a graphic artist, whose prints are imbued with great purity and superb technical control.

In the Cape interesting avant-garde work is being done by painters Kevin Atkinson (b. 1939) and Helmut Starke (b. 1936) and the sculptor Richard Wake (b. 1935). Their influence is formidable. Following their example, several young Cape artists such as Gerrit Hilhorst (b. 1945) and Jaco Kemp Bezuidenhout (b. 1941) are champing at the bit, throwing the staid traditionalists of that bland peninsula somewhat off balance.

In Durban, Patric O'Connor (b. 1940) and Andrew Verster (b. 1937) are the leaders. Their socially committed painting comments harshly on the decadence of the human species, and has caused a considerable stir among the normally complacent object of their irony.

Interesting art has emerged from the townships. Previously the South African Bantu had not expressed themselves through the medium of the visual arts to any great extent. The Zulus made beadwork. The Ndebele painted their huts. The rest of Bantu art was tourist art with little aesthetic value.

Today the Bantu artists fling their sheer life force with all its dramatic variations into their work. It bears no resemblance to indigenous African Folk art, but reflects daily

Sculptor Edoardo Villa's "Crusader" in forged steel (1962).

contact with European visual forms. Yet it is not European, but disturbingly ambiguous.

The most powerful of these artists is the sculptor, Sidney Kumalo (b. 1935). In his works one detects a knowledge of Western sculpture which is combined with a pure African vision that detects ancestral and evil spirits in each person, animal, plant and object encountered in daily life. Kumalo's figures are not only distorted in design, but heavy with latent emotion.

In complete contrast to the Bantu art of the cities, is the work of the Bantu at mission schools. Rorke's Drift is per-

Cecil Skotness
working on a giant woodcut.

haps the best-known center where graphic work, tapestries and pottery are made. The works are uncomplicated and enchanting, showing a naive and humorous interpretation of daily life and, above all, the Bible stories.

Considering the South African art scene as a whole, one may conclude that our art has come of age. It emerged largely from a European background, but was formed and colored by the environment in which it grew. Thus, although it may fit in happily and unobtrusively into the pattern of twentieth-century Western art, it has its own characteristics which make it distinctive.

HANDICRAFTS

Those cultural relics of the past which tell of life in bygone eras, are today proudly preserved in museums throughout South Africa, side by side with the country's great wealth of ethnological, anthropological and paleontological material.

South Africa's oldest building, The Castle of the Cape of Good Hope, houses a fine collection of beautiful antiques — furniture, porcelain, copper-ware, silverware, and paintings. So, too, does the Africana Museum in Johannesburg which is by far the most comprehensive treasure house of cultural historical material in the country. Most of the other bigger centers also have sections of their museums especially devoted to cultural historical material.

South Africa jealously guards these articles that have been preserved since the country's earliest days. Many of them come from the East, as the Cape was the half way port on

Fine Cape silver by the 18th century craftsman John Townsend.

the sea routes between the East and the West. Other articles were brought by new colonists from the countries of their origin in Western Europe. As time went by many household articles had to be made locally to meet the demands of an ever increasing pioneering community geographically isolated from Europe. There was for instance the exquisite silverware made by the eighteenth century silversmiths and furniture made from indigenous woods. Many pieces of old Cape silver and furniture have fortunately been preserved.

With the passing of centuries a new indigenous culture in handicrafts has been developed. Today pottery, hand-made jewelry, tapestries and mosaics are very much a part not only of private homes but also of many public buildings.

Pottery

Pottery is a relatively young industry in South Africa and South African potters are still striving to establish a strong tradition in this field.

Yet remarkable progress has already been made, especially in the last decade when a number of talented individual potters have come to the fore.

ABOVE: A tiled mural produced by one of the ceramic studios of South Africa.

LEFT: Examples of the work of South African potters — jar and vase by Esias Bosch and casserole by Andrew Watford.

RIGHT: Esias Bosch the potter.

51

Pretoria jeweler
Erich Frey is one
of the well-known
South African jewelers
who works with
semi-precious stones,
set in silver or gold.
Examples shown here
were displayed
in Münich in 1971.

Jewelry

The interesting rock formations and geological structure of South Africa and South West Africa are rich in minerals formed by the evolutionary erosions of many centuries. The earth in Southern Africa yields great riches in precious metals such as gold and silver, and true gems such as diamonds, and to a lesser extent, emeralds, rubies and sapphires. But there is also a great variety of rock material from which beautiful and sometimes quite unusual stones, usually referred to as semi-precious stones, can be cut.

In recent years South Africans have become fully aware of the various uses of these stones and are showing a tremendous interest in the development of a local industry. To a great extent this is due to the arrival in South Africa, since the 1940's, of a number of highly skilled, talented jewelers from European countries.

With the technical skill and the variety of material at their disposal, and the inspiration for designs which they so often draw from nature's shapes or freaks, these people have given the gemstone industry its first real impetus. Today many born South Africans are also tied up with the production of gemstone jewelry — as jewelers, stone cutters or designers.

RIGHT: Maia Holm's
handmade brass-and-beads jewelry.

BOTTOM: Rings of gold and diamonds
created by
goldsmith H. Livshitz of Johannesburg.

Black costume jewelry always
attracts the eye.

Tapestry

In medieval times history was often portrayed through the medium of richly woven, finely detailed tapestries. This age-old art has been revived in modern South Africa to depict part of the country's rich and colorful history. Today a number of large colorful tapestries, representing the history of the Great Trek, adorn the country's biggest national monument, the Voortrekker Monument. A number of accomplished needlewomen took eight years to complete this set of tapestries.

In the new Provincial Building in Pretoria there is a triptych tapestry symbolizing different stages in a woman's life. These tapestries were worked according to the age-old Gobelin technique and executed from materials especially selected and designed to endure the test of time. Artist Bettie Cilliers-Barnard designed the tapestries.

Even in the great commercial concerns such as the different mining houses large tapestries form a part of the interior decorations. These tapestries, many of which symbolize the rich mineral resources, are mostly the work of Ernest Ullmann.

54

The tapestry in the Voortrekker (Pioneer) Monument, Pretoria, depicts a birthday celebration in the 1850's.

By using an appliqué technique, Ernest Ullmann created panels like this in a series on the peoples of South Africa.

Elk Bantu Arts and Crafts Centre — Rorke's Drift, Natal. Bantu tapestry.

Mosaic

This art form, initially introduced to this country by Armando Baldinelli in the early fifties, is today a popular from of mural decoration, either in private homes or as huge mural panels built into the walls of public buildings such as commercial banks, vast office blocks, mining and other large financial concerns. Mosaics have become a part of modern architectural design in South Africa.

Batik

"Batik" is an old Malay word used to describe a process for coloring fabrics and has its origin among the Dutch East-Indian natives. A design, drawn on fabric, is partially covered with melted wax and certain uncovered portions then dyed. The wax is then dissolved by ironing it out of the cloth and the process repeated, thereby coloring new areas.

This form of art has now been revived in South Africa and thus generated tremendous public interest. Artists Louis Steyn and Johan Coetzee are foremost exponents of this old and decorative form of art.

56

Batik: Johan Coetzee's "Musicians"

ABOVE: She has never heard of a potter's wheel, yet, she . . .

RIGHT: H. Ntuli - celebrated sculptor of clay figurines.

Bantu Handicrafts

Zulu woodcarver and examples of his work.

Ndebele woman in traditional dress busy with beadwork.

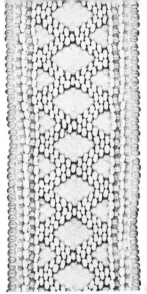

TOP: This Zulu woman nimbly handles a carpet loom in the Elk Bantu Arts and Crafts Centre at Rorke's Drift, Natal.

RIGHT: Traditional Bantu motifs are applied with equal success to modern dress design.

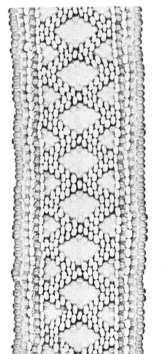

59

THE PERFORMING ARTS

Since the inception of provincial Councils for the Performing Arts in South Africa in 1963, a remarkable enlivement in the interest in opera, ballet, music and drama has taken place throughout the Republic of South Africa. Due to the almost overnight establishment of a secure professional habitat for the artist, the standard of all branches of the performing arts has blossomed; the public of South Africa, after years of lukewarm interest in these arts, has now come to the fore as a huge hitherto untapped force of "living audience", demanding performances of the best professional standards only.

With the blessing — and, of course, the financial aid — of the Government and the provincial and local authorities, the Performing Arts Councils of the Cape, Transvaal, the Free State and Natal became exciting arts industries, providing productions of plays in a bilingual country, and catering for the tastes and interests of the balletomane, the opera- and music-lover.

When the machinery of the Councils was put into motion, the idea was not to encroach on or tamper with the existing bodies providing commercial theatre, or with those specializing in importing concert artists, or with the established and admirable work done by the South African Broadcasting Corporation, or with the city orchestras in Cape Town and Durban. The subsidized PAC's were to render services where

Carel Trichardt as Shylock in "The Merchant of Venice". This play was produced in Afrikaans under the title "Die Koopman van Venesië".

Scene from the original South African ballet, "Mantis Moon", — based on a Bushman legend. Choreography: Frank Staff.

professional but financially non-aided undertakings could not do so on a profit-making basis. At the same time it was understood that the work done by amateurs should be regarded as something quite apart.

South Africa already had a background and a bit of a tradition in regard to drama. The touring companies of pioneers presented indigenous or translated plays in Afrikaans, and both local and imported companies staged English-language plays. These groups had to struggle across vast tracts of country to play in most inadequately appointed church, school and "town halls". Nevertheless, they established an interest in their art. The National Theatre Organization, established in 1947 and a forerunner of the Performing Arts Councils, helped to develop this interest and brought the theatre to a more professional standard. Thus the drama departments of the current bodies had at least some kind of foundation to build upon.

Not so with opera or ballet. Professional productions of opera were sometimes imported; the locally produced

Frank Staff —
a noted Choreographer.

Phyllis Spira and Gary Burne
— two of South Africa's
leading ballet dancers.

PACT Ballet rehearsal for "Sleeping
Beauty".

63

Tine Balder
as Mary in the Afrikaans production
of Eugene O'Neill's
"Long Day's Journey into Night".

Moliere's "Imaginary Invalid"
was performed by NAPAC in 1971.

operas were mostly by amateurs, bolstered by local or imported leads, but even for them there were hardly any full-time organizations arranging regular seasons.

The two larger Performing Arts Councils — PACT in Transvaal and CAPAB in the Cape — were the first to enter the arid operatic field in South Africa. They had to gather the artists from abroad and from South African sources and they did. Vocally, instrumentally, artistically and technically they have, in the past decade, produced operas comparable to those in some of the renowned opera houses in the world.

Some of the great names in the world of the opera now come to South Africa regularly to take part, as guest stars, in South African productions of a wide repertoire of opera. Cape Town was the first of the major South African cities to acquire a modern, magnificently-equipped opera house,

Scene from the indigenous South African ballet, RAKA. This ballet was based on a poem by N. P. van Wyk Louw.

venue of the major opera and ballet productions by CAPAB. Pretoria is next on the list: its new opera-and-theatre complex is expected to be completed by 1976 or '77. Other cities and towns will follow suit in the next decade.

Cape Town has had its ballet for more than thirty years. Johannesburg's permanent ballet company — previously the Johannesburg City Ballet — had been in existence a few years before the birth of PACT. Thousands of school-children are ballet students, but now, for the first time, the bright ones need not venture overseas to further their studies or seek careers as dancers: there are ample opportunities of becoming permanent members of South African ballet companies. The Cape and Transvaal ballet companies have attained such a high level in the last ten years that they could invite guest stars of the caliber of Dame Margot Fonteyn, Attilio Labis, Natalia Makarova, Ivan Nagy and Galina Samtsova to take part in their glittering productions.

LEFT: Lena (Yvonne Bryceland) cajoles the dying Outa (Sandy Tubé) in the film version of the play BOESMAN AND LENA by Athol Fugard.

Siegfried Mynhardt as Scapino.

But opera, ballet, drama and music are not for the metropolitan areas only. The outlying country districts are also served by touring companies, and schools are treated regularly to instructive, entertaining programs. The best available concert artists, small instrumental ensembles and even touring orchestras visit the country towns regularly. At least one internationally recognized group of musical artists is imported annually, to tour not only a single province, but all four. The Vienna Boys' Choir, the Münich Chamber Orchestra, the Salzburg Marionettes, the Paris Chamber Orchestra and the Ensemble Vocal de Lausanne have performed in South Africa under the auspices of the Performing Arts Councils.

The major symphony orchestra in South Africa is that of the S.A.B.C. Cape Town and Durban have their Civic Orchestras, while PACT and CAPAB maintain their own,

Mangalelwa Nyawose,
leader of the Zulu Impi
from the play
'UMABATHA' by Welcome Msomi.

fully established orchestras for operatic and ballet work, and also for concerts throughout the provinces.

Although works representative of the best classical and modern repertoire are being presented by the Performing Arts Councils, these bodies are being utilized for the performance of indigenous works. South African playwrights, choreographers and composers are encouraged or commissioned to create new works for presentation on the fully professional stage — the early harvests fully justify the creation of these facilities.

With this live, throbbing, thriving material at hand, South Africa, with the Performing Arts Councils working on a huge project of bringing the professional stage arts to the general public and to the schools of the country, and supplemented by the commercial organizations, is on the threshold of an era of cultural development. A vast audience has been born, and the artist is being given a place in the sun.

Dr. Anton Hartman, of the South African Broadcasting Corporation, conducting.

MUSIC

The major symphony orchestra in South Africa is that of the S.A.B.C. in Johannesburg — Cape Town and Durban have their Civic Orchestras and PACT created its own 60 piece orchestra — mainly for operatic and ballet work, but also for concerts throughout the province. In addition, the S.A.B.C. has also established its own Junior Symphony Orchestra under the baton of Walter Mony.

The interest in music in South Africa was for many years mainly stimulated by visiting musicians, conductors and opera and ballet groups from overseas.

The teaching of music was done according to the British Examination System, that of the Trinity College. In 1905 a Conservatoire of Music was established in Stellenbosch and followed by the S.A. College of Music in Cape Town in 1910. Eventually both institutions were absorbed in the Music Departments of the local Universities, and at present all the South African universities have established faculties of music.

Symphony orchestras exist in Cape Town, Durban, Johannesburg and Pretoria, the one in Johannesburg being that of the S.A.B.C. Besides the full-time conductors, Dr. Anton Hartman, Edgar Cree, David Tidboald, Francesco Mander and Leo Quayle, these orchestras are regularly conducted by visiting artists such as Willem van Otterloo, Daniel Sternefeld, Pierre Boulez, Franco Ferraris, Pierino Gamba, Antal Dorati, Hugo Rignold and Carl Melles.

Performances by the famous pianists Georges Themeli, Pierre Fournier, Julius Katchen, Hans Richter-Haaser and distinguished violinists, Alfredo Campoli, Christian Ferras and Robert Gerle were appreciated as much by South African audiences as abroad.

The Netherlands Chamber Choir under Felix de Nobel, the Hungarian String Quartette, the Munich Choir, Stuttgart Chamber Orchestra and the Berlin Philharmonic Octet are but a few of the famous groups of artists who had highly successful tours in South Africa.

As a result of the improved training facilities and bursaries allocated for overseas studies, South Africa has a number of composers who can be favorably compared with their colleagues in Europe and the U.S.A. The majority of South African composers have worked in London, Amsterdam, Boston or Vienna and are well-informed on the changing currents in contemporary music.

A member of a South African Orchestra.

Members of the PACT symphony orchestra — conductor Leo Quayle.

Of the contemporary South African composers, the best known is certainly Arnold van Wyk (born 1916). In 1938 he was awarded a bursary by the Performing Rights Society to study at the Royal Academy in London. At the same time he worked for the BBC. His first symphony was premiered by the late Sir Henry Wood in 1943 and repeated at the Cheltenham Festival in 1951. His other works have been performed successfully at international festivals of contemporary music e.g. his "Five Elegies for String Quartette"

Youth orchestras in South Africa stimulate early interest in serious music.

in Brussels in 1950. His song-cycle "Van Liefde en Verlatenheid" (Of Love and Forsakenness, words by Eugéne Nielen Marais) won an award at the International Festival in Israel in 1955. The Vienna Radio Orchestra and also the Nordwest-Deutscher Rundfunk Orchestra of Hamburg have given performances of his Second Symphony. He is the composer of one of the finest pieces of choral music to be created in South Africa: the "Kerskantate" (Christmas Cantata) with a strong Biblical flavor. His most impressive piano work "Night Music", completed in 1958, was appreciated by the English critic, Malcolm Rayment in "Music and Musicians" as "one of the most important contributions of our time to the literature of song". The British pianist, John Clegg, recently included this work in a piano recital in London.

Arnold van Wyk's latest compositions include "Masquerade, 7 symphonic movements" (1963-4); "Five Petronius Songs," for baritone and instruments (1959-1964), "Ou Paradys" (Old Paradise, words by C. Louis Leipoldt), 9 pieces for choir — a cappella (1964) and "Four Pieces for Piano" (Dumka, Scherzino, Romanza, Toccata), 1965.

Until recently, Mr. van Wyk lectured at the Cape Town College of Music. He is now lecturer in Music at the Conservatoire of Stellenbosch.

South African composer Arnold van Wyk.

Composer Stefans Grové
and his family.

John Joubert —
South African composer.

Another Cape composer is Hubert du Plessis (born 1922), whose work is known in Europe. His "Sonata for Piano Duet, Opus 10", was selected for the World Music Festival at Stockholm in 1956. Many of his works have been published in London and include vocal works for soloists and chorus as well as piano compositions.

John Joubert, born in 1927, entered the Royal Academy on a Performing Rights Society Scholarship and won the Royal Philharmonic Prize in open competition. His "Opus 20" was performed by the Birmingham University's Barber Institute of Fine Arts.

Like John Joubert, Stefans Grové, born in 1922, is another South African composer who worked abroad. He lectured at the Peabody Conservatory in Baltimore, Maryland. His works include "Divertimento for Woodwind" and "Symphonie Concertanto". He returned to South Africa in 1972.

Rosa Nepgen (born 1909) and Blanche Gerstman (born 1910) have interested themselves mainly in vocal music, the first having written numerous songs, mainly to Afrikaans texts, and the latter songs and choral works. During her long association with the Cape Town orchestra, Blanche Gerstman also wrote some orchestral works and a notable violin sonata.

Among the younger composers, the names of Cromwell Everson, Stanley Glasser, Graham Newcater and Carl van Wyk should be mentioned.

Newcater, one of South Africa's youngest professional composers, has been acclaimed as "absolutely brilliant" since the performances of his Symphony No. 1 and his Symphony No. 2, the latter composed as Safca's contribution towards the 1966 Republic Festival. Also commissioned by Safca, Hubert du Plessis composed his work "Suid-Afrika — Nag en Daeraad" (South Africa — Night and Sunrise). During the Republic Festival in 1966, the "Symphony for a Chamber music ensemble" by the 22-year-old Carl van Wyk was performed for the first time in Cape Town.

Child prodigy — Marian Friedman.

Mimi Coertse — operatic soprano.

Pretoria-born conductor, Prof. Johan van der Merwe, won the Fourth International Conductors' Competition organized by the Royal Liverpool Philharmonic Orchestra and had his first engagement with the orchestra on August 16, 1966. In 1972, Professor van der Merwe was appointed leader of the newly-formed symphony orchestra of the University of Pretoria.

The post-war compositions consist of spiritual and worldly music, vocal and instrumental or a combination of both. The traditional folk dance music ("boeremusiek") had no important influence on serious contemporary music. It is rather the choice of subject and the use of the Afrikaans verse in vocal works that might give the impression that South African music is different from the music of Europe e.g. "Van Liefde en Verlatenheid" (Of Love and Forsakenness) by Arnold van Wyk, "Die dans van die Rëen" (The Dance of the Rain) and "Slamse Beelde" (Malayan Images) by

Gert Potgieter — tenor.

Gé Korsten — tenor.

Joyce Barker — soprano.

Emma Renzi — mezzo soprano.

Hubert du Plessis, the humorous choir work based on "Klip-werk" (Stone Work) by the poet N. P. van Wyk Louw by Rosa Nepgen and "In die Droogte" (In the Drought), an opera by John Joubert.

South African music of this century is essentially a music in the tradition of Western Europe, but finding a new spiritual content in the experience of life and its peculiar tensions in the Southern African context.

Folk dancing to the rhythm of Boeremusiek in front of a Cape Dutch house.

IN LIGHTER VEIN

Folk dancers performing traditional dances in the open air.

Boeremusiek

The word "Boeremusiek" literally translated would mean "Farmers' Music." This however is not quite the case. Afrikaans speaking South Africans often refer to themselves as "Boere" because, before the tremendous development of the natural resources, industries and subsequent urbanization, the Afrikaans speaking people were primarily farmers. Boeremusiek therefore really means a distinct type of Afrikaans music. (Afrikaans "light" music is however no different from any other light music in the world and must not be confused with "Boeremusiek.") Through the centuries Boeremusiek, which is also light and danceable, has retained its own

79

peculiar style and color and uses only a traditional combination of instruments.

Because of the religious background, nearly every household of earlier Afrikaans-speaking South Africa, owned a harmonium or pedal organ which was used at evening prayers. This instrument plus a concertina and guitar, formed the basis of the Boeremusiek combinations. Because an accordion is easier to handle and transport, this instrument has replaced the harmonium to a large extent. It is also on record that the first accordion was used by the Voortrekkers (pioneers) during their long trek from the Cape to the Orange Free State, Transvaal and Natal. One can imagine the long and tiresome trek of over a thousand miles by ox-wagon over perilous mountains and dangerous rivers to the hinterland and the spontaneous moments of relaxation when the Voortrekkers sat on their wagons with accordion, guitar and concertina and sang folksongs to match their mood. These songs were either brought with them from their various countries of origin such as Holland, Germany or France with words in most cases adapted to suit local interests, or new words were made for the known melodies. Brand new melodies and words were also created by the more talented Afrikaans-speaking South Africans.

Boeremusiek can perhaps be best explained if compared with traditional or Dixieland jazz. This form of jazz has remained unchanged. This is also the case with Boeremusiek which is in fact "traditional Afrikaans music." Its rhythm is peculiar to itself, it has a color very much its own and most important, Boeremusiek still has a very large following in South Africa. The first Boeremusiek combination on record was performed during the 1850's. Today, at large "volksfeeste" when the nation swings into festive spirit, at private braaivleis parties (barbecues) or while relaxing around a campfire in the game preserves or on the beach resorts in Natal or the Cape, the accordion, concertina and guitar is invariably used to make music the South African way. Our

A typical South African barbecue (braaivleis).

folk dance groups have also through the years, cultivated a continuous interest in Boeremusiek by singing and dancing to its melodies. One of the most popular and widely used songbooks is the F.A.K.-Sangbundel (Songbook of the Federation of Afrikaans Cultural Societies). The newest edition features a selection of three hundred and eighty-eight songs, most of which is traditional Boeremusiek. Apart from over two thousand records released through the years of popular Boeremusiek, the Federation has now also started with their F.A.K. Record Club which is intended to acquaint today's generation with both contemporary and traditional Afrikaans music. Apart from this, a valuable contribution for the preservation of Boeremusiek is being made by the South African Broadcasting Corporation which, with never ceasing vigor, collects and makes recordings of the folksongs and folk music of yesteryear. Many private individuals have also made it their life task to visit elderly folk requesting them to play or sing some of the songs so they can be written down.

Folk Dancing

They came from bonny banks and braes . . . children in traditional Scottish costumes are put through their paces.

ABOVE: Portuguese dancers in national costume.

RIGHT: Two Coloured children in carnival dress. New Year's Day is a festive day for the whole Coloured community of Cape Town.

BELOW: A group of dancers getting ready to perform a Greek folk dance. The large and prosperous South African Greek community celebrates an annual Wine Festival with Greek folk dances.

FT: Zulu dancers.

ABOVE: Two young South Africans in Welsh costumes. In 1820 the first large contingent of settlers from the British Isles came to make sunny South Africa their home.

LEFT: A member of a Russian dance ensemble on stage at the Johannesburg Civic Theatre.

FAR LEFT: Members of the "Spanish Dance Theatre" on stage.

85

The calabash flute is used as solo instrument to while away the hours.

Bantu Music

Bantu Music in South Africa has many facets — the traditional, the light vocal, the instrumental, the choral, the hymnal and jazz.

The Bantu peoples of South Africa brought their traditional music with them from Central Africa. Here, in the South, in predominantly open plains, their folk music has become almost exclusively choral. The most popular form of singing among them is that of leader and chorus, the chorus part retaining a definite format and word content while the leaders, chosen for their ability with words, engender the character, flow and sparkle to the song as a whole, in a leading role

LEFT: A violin-type one-string bow — the companion instrument of the Tswana herdsman.

which might consist of an impromptu flow of words possibly including topicalities, or a quick recitative or praise or, in direct contrast, an epic historical narrative with choral interpollations on cue.

Some Bantu peoples have a classical song repertoire in which valorous deeds of past heroes and chiefs live on down the ages; they are subject to the strict censureship of their listeners who will not tolerate inaccuracies on the part of tribal bards. On the other hand there are hundreds of Bantu songs which are short lived and reflect the comings and goings of village life, the Bantu women, especially, bringing everything into song including comment or household grudge, safe from male retribution as they sing.

Bantu singing is inevitably coupled to movement, whether in work or in dance. Singing and dancing are accompanied by some form of rhythmic emphasis whether it be hand-clapping, heel stamping, the pounding of feet, the periodic clash of asegai on shield, or the beating of the drum. Tuned in sets, drums will produce tonal variety and cross rhythm; played either with the heel/palm/fingers of the hands, or in the case of the larger drums, with a stick flattened at the end to preserve the drum-head.

With Bantu words depending for their correct meaning on the exact tones in which they are spoken, song melodies reflect the individual characteristics of the ebb and flow and stresses of the different Bantu languages. Tonality has developed a distinctive traditional song repertoire in each of the Bantu peoples of South Africa, the Zulu, Xhosa, Southern Sotho, Northern Sotho, Tswana, Venda, Tsonga, Swazi, Ndebele.

Each Bantu nation has its quota of agricultural songs with songs for rain more prominent where the country is partial to drought. Initiation songs prevail where these schools continue to be tribally upheld. Songs of Bantu men tell of hunting exploits and recall a regimental warrior past. Zulu men, particularly, have a host of poignant courting songs. Songs abound. With the Bantu song a natural interflow of voice part is inborn.

Bantu singing has not been influenced by the melodies or harmonies of Bantu traditional instruments. Drums are played by the Northern Sotho, Tsonga and Venda peoples who live in the northern areas where trees of suitable girth for drum-

LEFT: Bantu jazz musician Pat Matsoapong, leader of the Katanga Jazz Men.

shells are to be found. Bów varieties, some with a calabash attached to the bow itself or the mouth used as resonating chamber, are prevalent. Light and easy to carry, they are solo instruments of the individual to while away the hours. A violin-type one-string bow is essentially the companion instrument of the Tswana herdsman as he watches over his cattle by day or by night at his solitary cattle-post. Tsonga and Venda players have adopted the wooden-slatted TIMBILA xylophone of the Mozambique Chopi people. The tinkling tones of the metal-tongued MBILA finger-piano or the Jew's Harp played by a young Bantu man or woman on a journey are often heard in the Northern Transvaal.

Reed flute ensembles — flutes of different lengths which each yield only the one note of their manufacture — flourish among Northern Sotho, Tswana and Venda young men. With TIMBILA, these are played in the Venda national TSHIKONA

An isolated horn is still blown at a festivity of tribal importance.

A township jazz group.

which is heard on all auspicious Venda tribal occasions. Only the MBILA and the TIMBILA have melodic range. An isolated horn is still blown at a festivity of tribal import, or, as in days of old when inter-tribal warfare was the order of the day, to summon the men to the chief's place.

Bantu men brought the melodic, harmonic and rhythmic essentials of their traditional music into the orbit of the penny-whistle, saxophone, guitar, double-bass and jazz drum world they found in the towns. From this combination there emerged TOWNSHIP (BANTU) JAZZ, an artistic form very melodically limited but essentially vibrating. Bands mushroomed as their weekend demand at parties grew and the record industry capitalized on this potential. In varying guises . . . Township Jazz, Saxophone Jive, Soul . . . continue to be top favorites among Bantu urbanites.

Using the Bantu-Jazz band as backing, and functioning on the same concert and record-selling lines, the light-vocal team of first four men, then four women, with or without male lead, has emerged to cater for essentially Bantu urban taste. The young Bantu women have dynamic platform appeal in their eye-catching attire with precision gymnastics which they perform as part of their singing act. They tour extensively throughout the Bantu areas of South Africa and in neighboring territories plugging their current record hits and often appear in films. They live highly, they dress well. They are the idols of Bantu teenagers.

In a completely different musical direction, the Bantu in South Africa, at schools and colleges, were trained by European teachers to sing Western hymns and choral works, in 4 part harmony, from Tonic Solfa notation. This produced a persistent line of Bantu hymn writers and religious and secular composers in Western image and a consequent growing awareness and love of choir singing in the vernacular, English, Afrikaans, even German and Italian, among the Bantu, old and young alike, throughout South Africa.

The focal point in Music teaching at Bantu schools is singing. Each Bantu Primary School has its Senior, Intermediate and Junior Choirs, each Bantu Secondary or High School and Training College has its choir. There are teacher choirs. They compete assiduously in Inter-School Choir Competitions which take place on a regional and provincial basis and, biannually, at National level, choirs travel hundreds of miles in special buses to participate.

Every Bantu community, small and large, has its adult church choirs, its music clubs and societies. In the towns, these choirs regularly combine for oratorio performances of works by Handel, Haydn, Mendelssohn, Bach . . .

Bantu choir singing, and the resonance of the Bantu bass voice, are a continuous source of delight to the overseas visitor to South Africa, the choirs never losing their Bantu modality. Perhaps because of the interest shown by the overseas visitor in their traditional music, several Bantu choirs, today, also include in their repertoire choral arrange-

The leader of the Soweto Symphony Orchestra, Mr. Michael Masoti (right), with a member of the orchestra.

ments of their indigenous songs. A handful of Bantu composers have given Western choral treatment to actual folk songs. One Xhosa composer has periodically interpollated a section of a well-known Xhosa folk-song as 'Xhosa quotes' in a choral work of his. There are also isolated choral compositions in which Bantu composers have used their indigenous musical idiom with great success. But no objective re-assessment of the composition possibilities of the indigenous folksong material at their disposal has made itself felt in Bantu choral composition to date.

There is, however, an awakening interest among the Bantu in South Africa in serious instrumental music. Apart from a handful of classical instrumental compositions by Sotho com-

The Ionian Choir with their conductor, Khabi Mngoma (photo: *The World*).

poser, Michael Moerane, and Zulu composer, Reuben Caluza, for Degree purposes, this interest was almost nonexistent until 1965 when Khabi Mngoma, as Recreation Officer of the City Council of Johannesburg for the Soweto Bantu township complex, with tremendous personal enthusiasm and considerable musical knowledge started musical theory and violin classes in Soweto. From his promising pupils he founded the Jubilee String Players and laid the foundation for the Soweto Symphony Orchestra which, today, has 50 players, fast becoming more and more proficient in their classical renderings. Dozens of other Bantu youngsters in Soweto attend weekly music classes and receive violin lesons under the auspices of the Johannesburg Bantu Affairs

Felicia Mabuza sings one of the songs from the musical "PHIRI", accompanied on the guitar by the composer Cyril Magubane.

Department. Staff notation is also taught in all Bantu schools in South Africa, and instrumental tuition given at Bantu training colleges.

South Africa has a long history of excellent Bantu brass bands . . . municipal, police, Salvation Army, railway . . . trained by professional European bandsmen. They supply any brass player requirements.

In earlier years there were also Bantu dance bands playing from orchestration. These older players were taught their instruments. Today, a group of young Bantu jazzmen are also determined to know their instruments. They have turned their backs on easy money and devoted themselves to the playing of progressive jazz, completely at home in the art of variation and improvisation which is so much a part of the Bantu traditional musical scene. Attuned to their 'natural' Bantu ear this jazz has an excitingly different sound which has already made its mark. Bantu Jazz festivals are highlights. In 1972 a 3-day non-stop Jazz festival was held at Umgababa, a Bantu holiday resort on the South Coast of Natal. Bands did their thing in huge marquees to the sound of the waves while jazz fans had their jazz fill perched either in the tents or lying on the beach.

* * *

Every Bantu man, woman and child makes music in South Africa . . .it is part of their whole way of life and living . . . only some do it better than others.

A section of the Bantu Symphony Orchestra at a rehearsal *(photo: The World)*.

RADIO SOUTH AFRICA

South Africa is unique among the nations of the world. Within its borders are many races and nations each with its own culture and traditions. It is a land restless for progress, a stirring giant striving to develop every aspect of its economic and cultural potential.

For thirty-six years the South African Broadcasting Corporation (SABC) has devoted itself to entertaining, enlightening and educating the peoples of South Africa. From a modest beginning in 1936 when only one program service was in operation in English with one hour per week for an Afrikaans program, the SABC has expanded to nineteen separate program services. These nineteen services are on the air for a total of 1,936 hours a week.

Radio programs in South Africa are broadcast in nine of the indigenous languages. For the Whites there are eight program services in one or both of the two official languages, English and Afrikaans. For the South African Bantu, seven program services in seven languages are provided, and for the indigenous peoples of South West Africa, there are three different language services.

The English Service broadcasts only in this language and is on the air for 120 hours a week. The Afrikaans Service caters for those whose home language is Afrikaans for the same number of hours a week. Springbok Radio is a bilingual commercial service and is on the air for 132 hours each week. These three services are broadcast on medium wave, short wave and VHF/FM.

Three special VHF/FM services also exist, namely Radio Highveld, Radio Good Hope and Radio Port Natal. The

RIGHT: Kathleen Davydd, (right) producer and Betty Mischeiker, (left) author, won the Japan prize during 1972 for a children's program on the English service.

BELOW: Radio Bantu, which is responsible for broadcasting to seven different Bantu language groups, carries a full entertainment service with newscasts, plays, talks, religious broadcasts, children's programs, women's features, sports broadcasts, quiz and variety shows and musical programs. Here announcer Mandla Sibiya is seen producing a play.

BELOW, RIGHT: Interview for Radio R.S.A. (French service).

first is confined to parts of the Transvaal and the Orange Free State, Radio Good Hope can only be heard in the south-western and eastern part of the Cape Province, while Radio Port Natal covers the Natal region. For 132 hours a week they each provide almost continuous music with news bulletins every hour. These stations use quarter- and half-minute spot advertisements which brings radio advertising within the reach of smaller business concerns that are not able to compete on the national network of Springbok Radio. Since the vast majority of South Africans are bilingual these special VHF/FM services use both English and Afrikaans throughout the day.

The eighth program service for Whites is called Radio South Africa and it brings bilingual radio entertainment to listeners from midnight to 5 a.m.

Each Bantu language group in South Africa enjoys a program service in its respective language. They are: The Zulu service which can be heard in Natal and the southern and south-eastern Transvaal; the South Sotho service broadcasts to the Bantu of that language group in the Orange Free State and the southern Transvaal; and the Xhosa service for the Xhosas of the Cape Province. These program services are on the air for 124½ hours per week.

The North Sotho service and the Tswana service each broadcasts for 89 hours 50 minutes a week. The former caters for the Bantu of that language group in the northern and central Transvaal while the latter is confined to the western Transvaal and the western Orange Free State. The Venda and the Tsonga services bring radio entertainment to these two language groups in the extreme north and north eastern Transvaal.

These services in seven languages are collectively known as Radio Bantu and all are broadcast on interference-free VHF/FM.

Radio Bantu is staffed with Bantu announcers, program compilers, clerks and disc jockeys. The popularity of Radio Bantu is best gauged by the volume of correspondence that

TOP: Stanford Mlaba and Patience Afrika as "Zeus en Athene".

CENTER: Announcer Abet Shiimi ya Shiimi of the Owambo Service.

BOTTOM: Heinrich Marnitz, announcer on the Afrikaans Service of the South African Broadcasting Corporation.

100

inundates Broadcast House each year. In 1962, 332,302 letters were received from Bantu listeners while in later years this figure rose to over 6 million letters in one year.

Radio Bantu programs include news bulletins, newsreels, talks, religious broadcasts, plays and serials, children's and women's features, daily school broadcasts, programs for old people, quiz contests and discussion programs, features, musical programs of all types, agricultural and gardening features, request programs, sport broadcasts and competitions.

The indigenous services for South West Africa which were introduced towards the end of 1969, experienced a period of solid growth and progress, particularly in the variety and quality of programs presented.

The three services known as Radio Herero, Radio Owambo and Radio Damara/Nama, are on the air daily for a total period of 19 hours. The Owambo Service broadcasts in Kwanyama and Ndonga for 9½ hours per day and the other two for 4¾ hours each.

The English service caters for the "conscious listener", in that the programs broadcast cannot be classified as "background". These programs cover all facets of modern radio entertainment with emphasis on the appeal and attraction that the program material will have for the discriminating listener. In this way the English service aims at providing programs for an ever-changing minority of listeners who want to hear some particular radio program or feature.

The Afrikaans service provides much the same sort of radio entertainment for the Afrikaans-speaking section of the community but musical programs that provide "background" are also included. The programs of both the Afrikaans and the English services are of a more cultural and informative nature than those that feature on the advertising services.

Springbok Radio, the main advertising service of the South African Broadcasting Corporation, relies on lighter radio entertainment. The programs on this service are

Record librarian, H. Kolatsoue (Johannesburg) assistant Rev. S. Phara to select hymns for his broadcast.

predominantly dramatic plays, serials, light music, competitions, quizzes and attractive news bulletins at peak listening times. This service is particularly popular with younger South Africans who are devotees of modern "pop" music and housewives who require light radio entertainment during the day.

Radio Highveld, Radio Good Hope and Radio Port Natal provide continuous musical entertainment throughout the day for those who do not care for speech programs. The music is classified as "middle of the road" and is neither too heavy nor too light. Advertising spots on these services are short and widely spaced so as not to break the musical continuity. Concise, pithy news bulletins are broadcast every hour, on the half hour, alternating in English and Afrikaans.

Radio South Africa, from midnight to five a.m. brings music, brief advertising announcements and messages to those South Africans who are engaged in night work. This service is extremely popular among its listeners who find that their unusual working hours are made more pleasant and bearable when "shared" with the announcer on duty.

Lourenço Marques Radio: This station is owned by the Radio Club of Mocambique but the youth oriented programs and advertising service are managed by the SABC. It broadcasts nationwide on shortwave and medium wave for 168 hours per week.

The External Services: Radio RSA, the Voice of South Africa, is the SABC's External Shortwave Service. It was born on 1st May, 1966 — to serve as an instrument of goodwill and to present a factual and objective account of all aspects of life in South Africa. RSA is an ambassador seeking to strengthen old friendships, to create new ties, to ask the world to pause and consider before accepting the comments of our critics and enemies. Dignity, objectivity and restraint are the characteristics of RSA's broadcasts.

Radio RSA offers what is acknowledged as one of the most topical, reliable and objective news services on shortwave. It is widely accepted as the authentic voice on South African events.

Programs are offered for 28 hours per day in nine languages — English, Afrikaans, German, Dutch, French, Portuguese, Swahili, Chichewa and Tsonga — and reception is good throughout the world. Four 250 kilowatt transmitters ensure that South Africa's voice is clearly heard in Africa, Europe, Australasia and North America.

What RSA offers has been most favorably received. The huge annual volume of correspondence and RSA's position in polls conducted among shortwave listeners attest to the station's popularity. All transmissions include news bulletins, brief editorial comment and programs designed to depict all aspects of life in South Africa. There are features on wildlife, tourism, indigenous music — both Bantu music and "Boeremusiek" have found wide appeal — discussion programs, magazine programs providing background to the headlines, and a variety of programs designed to reflect economic progress, the development of the Bantu Homelands, and to illustrate South Africa's history and potential. RSA offers facts — but facts attractively clothed, for although the programs are designed to inform, to build bridges, they must first and foremost provide good listening.

LEFT: Model of new buildings in Johannesburg. RIGHT: The new TV complex is nearing completion.

Windhoek, South West Africa.

The S.A.B.C. in Durban.

TOP: The studios
of Radio Bantu's
Xhosa service at
King Williams Town.

RIGHT: The
S.A.B.C. building
in Cape Town.

105

The SABC's Overseas Transcription Service forms part of its External Services and provides programs of a high technical and artistic standard to radio stations all over the world. The programs, which offer a wide variety of material, have been enthusiastically received by broadcasters and listeners alike.

The SABC National Symphony Orchestra, based in Johannesburg is the only full-strength symphony orchestra in South Africa. Eighty musicians and two resident conductors are employed full-time by the South African Broadcasting Corporation to provide symphony and lunch hour concerts for all members of the community. Periodic tours are undertaken by the orchestra to bring "live" concerts to other centers in the Republic other than Johannesburg. All concerts are recorded and broadcast later over the national network of the English or the Afrikaans Services.

Internationally famous soloists and conductors appear with the SABC Symphony Orchestra every year during its symphony seasons. During 1965 the visiting conductors were Pierre Boulez and Franco Mannino. During the same year artists from abroad included the pianists Georges Themeli, Peter Frankl, Eric Heidsieck, Sergio Varella-Cid, Abbey Simon, Michel Block and Claude Coppens; the violinists Christian Ferras, Alfredo Campoli and Marcel Debot; the 'cellist Andre Navarra; the Endres Quartet, the Quarteto Classico di Madrid, the Lucerne Festival Strings, the Vienna Boys' Choir and the organist Michael Schneider.

Every year brings greater development and progress for the South African Broadcasting Corporation in its striving to provide not only top quality programs but also the best possible reception in a country, the topography of which is most unsuited for reliable radio propagation. This policy of the SABC which calls for the best in programing and equipment ensures that every individual in the Republic of South Africa will benefit and in so doing make his contribution to the success and welfare of the entire country.

In April 1971, the South African Government accepted

The National Symphony Orchestra of the South African Broadcasting Corporation.

the Report of the Commission of Inquiry into Matters Relating to Television in its essentials and approved in principle the introduction of a statutorily controlled television service for South Africa, to form an integral part of the Republic's broad educational system as a whole and based on a foundation designed to ensure that the Christian values of the Republic of South Africa and the social structure of all its various communities are respected. The entrust of the establishment and furtherance of the service to the SABC added substantial momentum to the Corporation's great forward surge and consequently increased the SABC's responsibilities even further.

As a first step, the SABC appointed its own Television Project Committee, consisting of some of the most senior officials in the organization. A team of consultants was then

This 600 ft. tower at Brixton, Johannesburg, is topped with a 160 ft. steel mast which carries the antennae for the South African Broadcasting Corporation's Frequency Modulation services.

A technician repairs a turntable amplifier in the workshop.

appointed under the leadership of the SABC's Television Project Committee.

The so-called Phase 1 of the television service is presently planned to commence scheduled broadcasts in January, 1976, and will consist of one channel, devoting 37½ hours weekly, during the late afternoons and evenings, equally to the Afrikaans and English languages.

The television complex in Johannesburg, planned to be the major television production facility of the SABC, is presently being erected on a site adjacent to the SABC's new radio complex and is already in an advanced stage of development.

This television complex, which will comprise approximately 525,000 square feet of floor space in Phase 1, consists of all the necessary technical facilities, 7 studios, an artists' block as well as facilities for scenery manufacturing, pre-assembly and storage. Provision has also been made for expansion in future phases of development.

Eighteen television transmitter stations are to be erected in Phase 1, covering all the densely populated areas of the country and these stations will provide nearly 80% of the country's population with television reception from the outset.

It is possible that limited production facilities will also be provided in Phase 1 in Cape Town and the necessary facilities will be built to house terminal and Post Office equipment at strategic points throughout the country where SABC radio studio facilities are already in existence. Simultaneously, certain renovations to and replacement of existing radio buildings will be effected in some of these centers.

At Pietersburg, in the Northern Transvaal, a new radio studio building is to be erected in the near future for the Northern Sotho, Tsonga and Venda Bantu language groups respectively.

A new building, comprising some 25,000 square feet, is presently being erected in Bloemfontein, Orange Free State, to accommodate the SABC's radio and television activities in that city, whilst in Port Elizabeth, Eastern Cape, a building will be erected in order to provide additional accommodation and studio facilities.

The SABC will need more than a thousand additional employees for Phase 1 of its television service and a small number of these posts will have to be filled from abroad.

An extensive training program has already commenced in the SABC's own Television Training Centre in Johannesburg.

The production of an episode in a Xhosa serial with some members of the cast in traditional tribal garb.

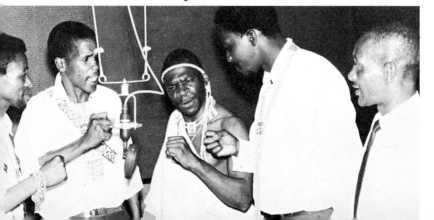

MOTION PICTURE INDUSTRY

A frame taken from one of the oldest political propaganda films, produced during the Anglo-Boer War, and entitled THE SET-TO BETWEEN JOHN BULL AND PAUL KRUGER.

The magical world of the cinema is not new to South Africa, for the Republic was one of the first countries in the world in which films were projected and produced.

The lure of diamonds and gold brought many thousands of Europeans and Americans to South Africa in the latter half of the previous century. To entertain these get-rich-quick adventurers, there were cabarets, music-halls, boxing, etc., and in 1895 the first films "Buffalo Bill", "A Cockfight" and "Carmelita performing a skirt dance", were shown in Johannesburg. At first a mere novelty, film-fever soon gripped the South African audiences, and in their thousands they streamed to these shows.

In 1896, Carl Hertz forcibly removed one of Robert Paul's projectors from the Alhambra Theatre in London and left with it the next day from Southampton for South Africa! So it happened that the very first film performance at sea was aboard the "Norman" given by Hertz en route to South Africa. Edgar Hyman, who was at the time manager of the Empire Palace of Varieties in Johannesburg (where Hertz was showing his films), was so impressed with this new medium, that he acquired a camera and started filming scenes in Johannesburg and around South Africa. So Hyman became the first newsreel cameraman in South Africa. Some of these early newsreel films have been traced and are now preserved by the National Film Board of the Republic of South Africa.

When war between Britain and the Boer Republics became inevitable in 1899, Hyman took his camera to Cape Town and filmed the first war newsreel in South Africa — the arrival of the British troops. With his two colleagues Stanford and Dickson, Hyman continued to film many scenes during the whole war.

They were joined in rapid succession by four other film units, Warwick Trading Company, British Biograph and Mutoscope Company, Robert Paul and Vitagraph from America, and so dozens of newsreels were shot during the Anglo-Boer War of 1899-1902.

But the war not only stimulated newsreel activity, it also saw the birth of the political propaganda film in South Africa. The first effort was called "The set-to between John Bull and Paul Kruger" and in it these characters are shown in a boxing match, with France and Russia as seconds to Paul Kruger and Uncle Sam in John Bull's corner.

The war further inspired the first war recruiting films, the first dramatic war movies and the first motion picture dealing with social problems caused by war. This event, therefore, did more to establish the cinema than is generally conceded. The screening of newsreels which started during this time, became a permanent weekly feature from 1911 on and

Early film-making by African Film Productions. The frame and cable above the actress' head is keeping the microphone in position.

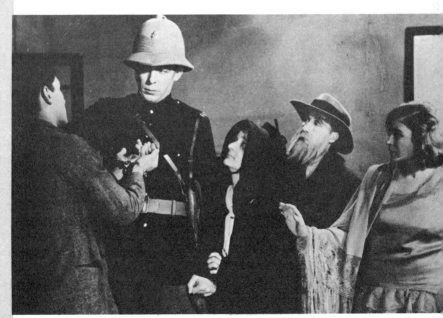

From left to right: Pierre de Wet, Carl Richter, Stephanie Faure, Plaat Stultjes and Joan du Toit in "Moedertjie".

makes "South African Mirror" one of the oldest newsreels in the world today.

The war firmly established motion pictures in South Africa. British as well as South African companies, aware of the wonderfully exotic nature of South Africa and her peoples, began to film many travel films for overseas distribution and permanent theatres were built for the showing of films. Soon there were too many theatres for the limited and comparatively small audiences of a still young country and many were forced to close down. It was feared that the whole entertainment structure was going to collapse, and so a call went out to the insurance financier, I. W. Schlesinger, to re-organize the film industry. Schlesinger was to become the uncrowned king of the industry for the next forty years. He negotiated the foundation of the companies that were to save the entertainment industry, and ensured the continuity of film production and distribution. One of his companies, African Film Trust, soon owned more than 50 cinemas throughout the country, and the other, African Film Productions, continued newsreel production and started with feature and documentary films. In 1916, the first film studio was built for A.F.P. in Killarney, just north of Johannesburg. This studio remained in continuous production until 1972. During 1916, A.F.P. alone made 13 feature films, one of which was "De Voortrekkers". This film was released overseas during the First World War with the title "Winning a Continent" and is mentioned in Kine-yearbook together with "Intolerance" of Griffith as one of the most important films of its time.

In 1929 the talkies came to South Africa with "Mr. Smith Wakes Up", and 1931 saw another important event for motion pictures in South Africa with the release of "Moedertjie" (Little Mother) — the first feature film with a sound track in Afrikaans. Joseph Albrecht from England, often called the father of film production in South Africa, directed this film and George Noble was the cameraman. "Moedertjie" and the members of its crew received the first

TOP: Dingaan's kraal in "De Voortrekkers".

BOTTOM: Adrian Steed, Johan du Plooy, Fred de Wet and Louis van Niekerk in "Pressure Burst". A Killarney Film Studios production.

Richard Daneel, director, Hymie Kirstein, producer and John Brown, director of photography. Hymie Kirstein son of pioneers of Johannesburg is himself one of the pioneers of the film industry in South Africa. For many years a managing director of Killarney Film Studios and producer of many important films. He not only won the first international prize for South Africa with his film "Zebediela" but was also responsible for many innovations in the film industry as well as training most of the leading film-makers working in South Africa today.

award dedicated to the film industry by the South African Academy of Arts and Science.

One would have expected a spate of South African feature films to compete with the ever growing number of American and British films shown at that time, but these were the years of the Depression, and it was not until the Second World War that studios once again started producing feature films. While they were not making features, African Film Productions and other companies like the Union Film Company, continued making documentaries, especially for the government, for overseas distribution. Of these "Golden Harvest", made by Joseph Albrecht, won an award at the Venice Festival in 1939.

Up to the Second World War, South Africa as part of the British Commonwealth, was to a large extent influenced by the British way of life. But the isolation of the war during the forties, forced South Africans to rely more on their own resources. For the first time Afrikaners financed, produced, wrote and made Afrikaans films. New companies like Vobi, RARO, Utolo and Union Films started producing features in Afrikaans. However, the drive of a really creative film-maker was missing — but not for long.

In 1953 Jamie Uys came in from the Transvaal Bushveld with a picture that he had made alone with his young wife, Hettie Uys. Jamie Uys not only brought a fresh approach to film-making, but also a rare and uncomplicated sense of visual humor. Uys became an immediate success with the public, spent some time with Killarney Film Studio,

LEFT: Jamie Uys and his son Wynand who played the leading part in "Lost in the Desert".

RIGHT: Jamie Uys as Rip in "Rip van Wyk".

Tom Meehan (Sir Gregory Pitkin) and Roger Service (Richard Lamb) in the 'General Assistance Department', a scene taken from "The Men from the Ministry" a Killarney Film Studios production.

Scene from the film "Die Kandidaat" by Emil Nofal Films. From left to right: Cobus Rossouw, Wilhelm Esterhuizen, Andries Roux, Jacques Loots, Gert van den Bergh, Marié du Toit and Hermien Domisse.

and then formed his own company — Jamie Uys Film Productions. Uys has the distinction that he pioneered bilingual films and co-productions with overseas companies for international release.

Through Jamie Uys Film Productions, South African film-making reached maturity with films made by Emil Nofal and Jans Rautenbach. Together they made "Wild Season" which ushered in a new era in motion pictures in South Africa. With productions such as "Wild Season", "Die Kandidaat" (The Candidate), and "Katrina", they were to prove that serious and well-directed locally produced films, devoid of cheap sentimentality, could be even more successful commercially than was first thought. Nofal has since made "The Winners" which was a tremendous box-office success and was acclaimed at Cannes in 1973.

In 1945 African Consolidated Theatres and African Film Productions (now called Killarney Film Studio) both part of the Schlesinger Organization, practically monopolized the film industry. Since then the pattern has changed considerably. Through the interest and capital investment of South Africans in this industry an indigenous organization, Ster Films, was formed. This group now owns almost as many cinemas and drive-in movies throughout the Republic as the Schlesinger Organization which has, however, recently

Gert van den Bergh as Antoine Rossouw in "The Second Sin".

Anna Neethling Pohl as Ouma (grandmother) du Toit in the screen version of the Stuart Cloete novel "Hill of Doves".

merged with the powerful Anglo-American Group. There are also about 300 independent outlets in cities and towns. New sound studios like Cavalier Films and Lone Hill have also been established and many smaller studios were opened in all the major cities.

There are presently over 80 registered film companies in existence producing advertising films, documentaries, and up to 24 features yearly. Apart from the local companies, several producers from overseas visited South Africa for filming purposes and movies such as "Creatures of the World Forgot" by Hammer Productions and "Zulu" by Stanley Baker were produced.

Although film-making is an established industry in South Africa, with experienced actors, technicians and directors, the country needs producers to provide the money to back films of a standard and quality which will make them competitive with world productions.

Until television is introduced in 1976, live theatre and the cinema will continue to provide the essential entertainment for people whether they live in cities or in the smaller towns that abound in the Republic. During the sixties, Ster Films began to prepare for the advent of television by building complexes which house several smaller but very luxurious cinemas, restaurants and ice-rinks, in all the major centers of the Republic. Today there are more than 600 four-wall and drive-in cinemas in South Africa, catering for the many peoples in the country.

An important event in the history of the South African motion picture industry was the establishment of the National Film Board in 1964. The Board undertakes to either make or tender out to the private sector, all the films required by the various government departments.

Circumstances are pointing to a bright future for the South African film industry. It is hoped that this will materialize and that the South African entertainment film will attain its rightful place with the South African documentary film in the international film sphere.

ARCHITECTURE

Union Buildings, Pretoria. (Architect: Sir Herbert Baker)

Architecture in South Africa, since the time of settlement, has always been "contemporary". Strategically located on the main route between East and West, it maintained direct contact with Europe and America, keeping abreast of developments in the larger countries through the technical personnel who made the Cape their port of call.

From the age of the great Dutch architects whose practice ranged between New Amsterdam, Stockholm and Batavia, to the age of Le Corbusier, architecture in South Africa reflected the current trend in a manner out of all proportion to its geographic remoteness and the size of its population.

The people showed great enterprise and a gift for improvisation in adapting the new ideas to their difficult sur-

Library of the Bantu University of the North, Transvaal.

roundings. Through the process of adaptation, distinctive characteristics emerged. While the works in any one period in South Africa can readily be identified with contemporary developments elsewhere, the country's architecture bears an individual stamp as strong as that which distinguishes French from Spanish, or Dutch from Italian buildings.

Overseas precedent and local initiative combine to make South Africa's contribution unique in the cultural heritage of the West.

From the outset, the architecture of the Cape was modelled on the strict classical ideas of Palladio, the grand garden designs of le Notre, and the fortification principles of Vauban. The Castle, the Company's Garden, and the Governor's residence established a pattern which was followed all the way down the line to the smallest farmhouse. When Governor Simon van der Stel and his son Adrian laid out their plantations at Groot Constantia and Vergelegen, Versailles provided the example. Sites commanding distant views were embellished with avenues of oaks, camphor trees, orchards and vineyards, all laid out in a regular fashion. The manor

122

These Ndebele houses display a different kind of architecture.

houses echoed the design of those in Holland, though their construction was more massive. Solid lime-plastered walls carried heavy wooden beams and high thatched roofs. These roofs sported ornamental gables in the styles prevalent in Amsterdam, but under the blue skies of the southern climate the great white gables attained a monumentality setting them apart from their Dutch prototypes. By extending the white walls and gateways from the house itself to the limits of the cultivated domain, the builders made a strong impression on the vast, dark and savage landscape.

The idyllic pastoral life of the interior was shattered by the discovery of minerals, the influx of immigrants, and the advent of the railroad. New building materials accompanied a new way of life from the industrialized countries, and new cities arose in a new style of architecture. For all of its rawness and brashness, this hybrid of the South African veld and overseas industry produced buildings of down-to-earth functionalism and vitality of form unmatched in later periods of greater sophistication. Englishmen in Natal, furthering the ideals of Morris, Voysey, and Mackintosh,

Groote Schuur hospital in Cape Town.

The wine cellar at Groot Constantia near Cape Town. The wine farm was founded by the Dutch Governor Simon van der Stel in 1685.

The entrance to the Castle. (Bowler print from Album of 12 published in 186(

124

Modern South African homes.

Germans in South West Africa intent on developing a logical response to an exotic climate, made common cause with the Dutch tradition to evolve a workmanlike architecture of brick and corrugated iron, characterized by spreading verandas and shady eaves.

A new generation, grown wealthy on the basic mining and secondary luxury industries, grafted embellishments in cast iron and moulded terracotta onto the no-nonsense buildings of the pioneers. In the ostrich-farming region around Oudtshoorn, which boomed after the Gay Nineties, veritable palaces arose sporting a riot of mechanical ornament. This was carried further in the growing cities, where more monumental structures of stone and marble arose in florid Flemish Renaissance Revival and Edwardian Baroque, with detailing in the current Art Nouveau style.

Cultivation of the hinterland supplied the port of Cape Town with supplies for passing ships, and townsfolk made a good living out of trade. This was reflected in the architecture. Travelers have commented favorably on their hospitality and its setting. In the hey-day of the late Rococo style, Cape Town's buildings presented a startling contrast to the sobriety of the country houses. Brightly colored facades, trimmed with undulating white cornices, surmounted by urns, balustrades and statuary, provided the backdrop for a way of life which earned for the town the name of "Little Paris".

Remote from the cosmopolitan port, frontiersmen on the high plateau of the interior developed a way of building more in keeping with their hard existence. Modest flat-roofed dwellings conceived in the most austere Palladian style, clustered around sober churches and stately avenues of oaks and cypress, bordered by irrigation canals. Trekking into the unknown, they carried on the traditions of the founders of the settlement in an architecture showing a remarkable affinity to the period with which they consciously identified themselves: the heroic age of the Biblical patriarchs.

Groote Schuur, Cape Town, official residence of the South African Prime Minister.

As Prime Minister of the Cape, mining magnate Cecil John Rhodes commissioned the young architect Herbert Baker to evolve a national style for public buildings. Baker restored several manor houses from the period following on the governors van der Stel, and based his Cape Dutch Revival Style on these examples. For more monumental structures he drew on precedents in the classical tradition of the Mediterranean countries. Over three decades spanning the act of Union in 1910, this style, officially adopted by the Public Works Department, served the country well for government buildings, hospitals, schools, and memorials.

127

LEFT: BP Centre, Cape Town's tallest building, is turned at an angle of 45° to the city grid, providing improved natural light, better views, and more efficient air conditioning. Precast concrete sunscreens shade the clear glass windows.

RIGHT: Heerengracht Building, Cape Town (incorporating offices and an hotel).

In the late twenties as young lecturer at the Witwatersrand University School of Architecture, Rex Martienssen, established contact with Le Corbusier and became a friend of Fernand Leger. At the same time, Gerard Moerdyk introduced the concepts of De Stijl in Holland to South African church buildings. As a result, the ideas of the European

Advanced technique used in constructing the Standard Bank building in Johannesburg.

avant-garde in architecture became acclimatized at an early date. For the next decade South Africa led the Commonwealth in applying the new functional approach to architectural problems. Experience was gained in the use of reinforced concrete and steel, preparing the building industry for the boom conditions generated by the industrial revolution after the Second World War.

A Muslim mosque lends an Eastern flavor to the South African scene.

The war both emphasized the interdependence of South Africa and the West, while throwing the country back on its own resources. Heavy and secondary industries were stimulated, urbanization accelerated, and a massive campaign of expansion and development undertaken. Six schools of architecture now meet the demand for trained men in the Republic. Close reciprocity with professional bodies overseas, and a regular exchange of educationalists ensure the maintenance of standards. Niklaus Pevsner and William Holford of Britain, Hentrich of Germany, Woods of France, Buckminster Fuller and Soltan of the United States are among the many leaders in this field who have recently visited the universities. A constant interchange of men and ideas characterizes the historical pattern of South African architecture as an integral part of the Western tradition.

The ultra-modern Randse Afrikaanse Universiteit.

Pretoria University, Administration building.

131

SPORT AND RECREATION

Horse riders amidst picturesque surroundings.

Mainly because South Africa has a mild to hot climate and sunny days during most of the year, it is a land of the out-of-doors. A study of sport and outdoor recreation in South Africa thus provides proof in yet another way of the many possibilities to be found in this country. While the challenge of river, mountains, forests and wild-life still forms the basis of most recreational activities, sport is undoubtedly the most popular organized activity in the country. South Africans are well known for their international achievements in the sporting world.

Competitive sport in South Africa is organized on a club, provincial and national basis. There are 69 official national controlling bodies to which all provincial bodies and clubs are affiliated. These organized bodies provide ample opportunity for competitors to participate in sport at all levels,

RIGHT: A new South African record was established in the 1500m for women during South Africa's Open International Games 1973.

BELOW: Sally Little, winner of the individual section of the world golf tournament for women held in Madrid in October, 1970.

including international competition, either in South Africa or abroad. In addition, a government Department of Sports and Recreation was established in 1966 with the aim of promoting sport and recreation amongst all population groups. This department renders services and does not exercise control. Its services are available to all sports bodies in the form of both technical advice and subsidies. It assists, for example, in the training and coaching of sports leaders and participants in purchasing basic equipment, with international participation and in the improvement in the administration of sport in general.

The majority of South Africa's black population has only become interested in organized sport in recent years. To encourage their enthusiasm a program of construction of modern sport facilities was initiated and is rapidly overtaking that of the whites, thus allowing non-white sportsmen every possible opportunity of improving their standard of performance.

South African sportsmen selected to represent South Africa at the international level are known as Springboks. These men and women have over the years brought recognition and honor to South Africa in many sporting spheres. In such world events as the Olympic Games, South African athletes have proved their mettle and high standards of performance by winning many medals. In sports such as rugby and cricket, two of the most popular competitive games in South Africa, the Springboks have attained world recognition and captured many honors. On the tennis courts South African sportsmen and women have also gained international prestige. South Africa is a regular competitor in the Davis Cup and the Federation Cup competitions.

South Africa has many international sporting stars. The name of Gary Player, one of the few men in history of professional golf to have won the 'Grand Slam', is known to every person in the world interested in this sport. A new name in golf circles is Sally Little, winner of the 1970 Amateur World Championships. The wonder swimmer, Karen

Rugby: The Springboks versus
the All Blacks, 1970.

During 1970 a polo team from
the Argentine won 9 - 3 against
a Springbok team.

Cricket: Northern Transvaal versus Australia.

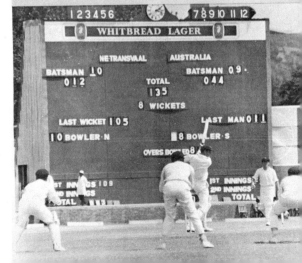

Water-skiing.

Surfing.

Muir, holder of several world backstroke records; Paul Nash, the sprinter who equaled the world 100-meters time of 10 seconds; and Gert Potgieter, holder of the world record over 400 meter hurdles, are only a few of the South African sportsmen who have competed successfully at the highest international levels. The outstanding achievement of Bruce Dalling in his 50-foot lightweight yacht in coming second and, in terms of handicap, being adjudged first in the international single handed Trans-Atlantic race, is another fine example of the sports potential of the Republic. The Cape to Rio yacht race has become a popular event and a trial of courage and endurance. In the field of motor racing South Africa has much to be proud of. The annual South African Grand Prix is internationally recognized and counts towards the world championship. Jody Scheckter has won many events and is currently South Africa's leading contributor to this exciting sport.

The Bantu people of South Africa have also made world standard contributions to sport. Some of the outstanding Bantu sportsmen are Humphrey Knozi and Benonie Malaka

Fresh water angling.

Gary Player, international golf star.

in the 800 meters, boxer Lukas Matseke, who won a gold medal at the United States Amateur Boxing Championships in 1963, and Henry Jones, the body builder who represented South Africa in the "Mr. Universe" contest.

In such lesser-known sports as Jukskei (similar to horse-shoe pitching), a traditional South African sport, men and women have undertaken several tours to the United States. Lawn Bowling is another favorite amongst the outdoor sports and South Africa hosted many nations to a recent world competition during the South African Games in 1973.

South Africans have a proud, hard-earned reputation in the world of sport — a reputation achieved by dedicated men and women. The interest which non-whites have developed in competitive sport, the fact that excellent facilities are available and that specialized attention is given to modern techniques, are reasons enough to believe that South Africa will in future do even better in the field of international sporting endeavor.

Most South Africans take full advantage of the climate by engaging in some or other form of open-air activity. Of

137

those recreational activities, horse-riding and angling are favorite pastimes. Weekend and holiday outings to mountains, rivers and seaside resorts are popular among the young and old alike. Camping and barbecuing (braaivleis) in natural forests and woods are as popular as ever. The inland waters are used extensively for canoeing, yachting and boating and water skiing is becoming increasingly popular.

South Africa's coastline does not only have an abundance of beautiful beaches but also provides some of the finest surfing and scuba diving in the world. Both of these popular sports are great pastimes and during 1973 South Africa hosted an international Surfboard Riding Competition.

. . . ship ahoy.

Bowling at the foot of Table Mountain.

"Jukskei", the all South African game being practiced by a young enthusiast during the National Competitions in 1970.

139

In 1973 South Africa was host to the world during the third South African Open International Games held in Pretoria, the administrative capital of the Republic. The first South African Sports Festival was staged in Johannesburg as part of the Johannesburg Festival in 1959. In 1964 the first official South African Games were held at the Wanderers Stadium, Johannesburg. The second official South African Games were held in 1969 in Bloemfontein in the Orange Free State. More and more international athletes joined in these Games and during the 1973 event 673 competitors and officials representing 29 overseas countries participated in 31 sporting events. During the same Games 993 South Africans from all races competed against one another. The

The U.S. basketball team vs. South Africa during the Open International Games of 1973.

A Bantu sportsman in excellent form.

Competition is keen in the 400 metre hurdles.

major sports in which the blacks excelled were football, athletics and boxing.

During 1973 South Africa maintained its presence and high reputation in world sporting events. The Republic's sportsmen competed locally and outside the country in all but 10 of the 72 registered sports. Overseas they participated as official teams or as individual entries in 43 different types of sports.

In 1966 the State President's Sports Award was established in recognition of world-class performances by South Africans. This coveted award is presented annually as an incentive to sportsmen throughout the Republic to ensure that the highest standards of individual performances are maintained.

REFERENCE LIST

Alexander F. L.
Art in South Africa Since 1900,
A. A. Balkema, Cape Town

Atmore, M. G.
Cape Furniture,
Howard Timmins, Cape Town

Battiss, Walter
The Artists of the Rocks,
The Red Fawn Press, Pretoria

Berman, Esmé
Art and Artists of South Africa,
A. A. Balkema, Cape Town

Burman, Jose
Waters of the Western Cape,
Human & Rousseau, Cape Town

Calburn, Simon
Birds of South Africa,
Purnell and Sons, Cape Town

De Klerk, W. A.
The White Wines of South Africa,
A. A. Balkema, Cape Town

D'Oyly, Sir Charles
*The Cape Sketchbooks of Sir Charles
D'Oyly, 1832-1833*
A. A. Balkema, Cape Town

Eglington, Charles
Maud Sumner,
Purnell and Sons, Cape Town

Elliott, Arthur
*Architectural Beauty of the Old
Cape as seen by Arthur Elliott,*
A. A. Balkema, Cape Town
Entertaining with Cape Wines,
K. W. V., Paarl, S.A.

Fehr, William
Treasures at the Castle of Good Hope,
Nasionale Boekhandel, Cape Town

Fransen, H. and
Cook, M.
The Old Houses of the Cape,
A. A. Balkema, Cape Town

Gordon-Brown, A.
*Christopher Webb Smith, an Artist
at the Cape of Good Hope 1837-1839,*
Howard Timmins, Cape Town

Greig, D. E.	*Herbert Baker in South Africa* Purnell and Sons, Cape Town
Hatfield, Dennis	*Some South African Monuments,* Purnell and Sons, Cape Town
Huskisson, Yvonne	*The Bantu Composers of* *Southern Africa,* S. A. B. C., Johannesburg
Jeppe, Harold	*South African Artists,* Afrikaanse Pers Boekhandel, Pretoria
Kaplan, Alec	*Catalogue of the Coins of* *South Africa,* the Author, 311 Pan Africa House, Johannesburg
Labuschagne, Rudolph Johannes, *comp.*	*Our National Parks,* National Parks Board, Johannesburg
Lee, Dennis Neil	*Art on the Rocks of Southern Africa,* Purnell and Sons, Cape Town
Lewcock, R.	*Early Nineteenth Century Architecture* *in South Africa* A. A. Balkema, Cape Town
Manuel, George	*District Six,* Longmans (S.A.), Cape Town
Mertens, Alice	*Etosha, South West Africa,* Nasionale Boekhandel, Cape Town
Mulder, C. F. J.	*Five Hundred Years, A History of* *South Africa,* Academica, Pretoria
Opperman, D. J.	*Spirit of the Vine,* Human & Rousseau, Cape Town
	Our Art I and II: Publ. Journal Lantern in collaboration with S.A.B.C., Pretoria
Pama, C.	*Lions and Virgins,* Human & Rousseau, Kaapstad
Pearse, G. E.	*Eighteenth Century Architecture* *in South Africa,* B. T. Batsford Ltd., London

143

Pearse, G. E.

*Eighteenth Century Furniture
in South Africa,*
J. L. van Schaik, Pretoria

Picard, Hyman W. J.

*Gentleman's Walk, the Romantic story
of Cape Town's oldest streets, lanes
and squares,*
C. Struik, Cape Town

Picard, Hyman W. J.

*Grand Parade, the birth of Greater
Cape Town 1850-1913,*
C. Struik, Cape Town

Rosenthal, Eric

*Runner and Mailcoach, The history of
philately in South Africa,*
Purnell and Sons, Cape Town

*South Africa (Republic) Department
of Information: Groote Schuur,*
residence of South Africa's Prime
Minister. The Department of
Information, Pretoria

Scholtz, Merwe, *ed.*

Wine Country,
Buren, Cape Town

Tyrrell, Barbara

Tribal Peoples of Southern Africa,
Books of Africa, Cape Town

Ullman, Ernest

Design on Life
Howard Trimmins, Cape Town

van der Spuy, Kenneth Reid

Old Nectar and Roses, Books of Africa,
Cape Town
Twentieth Century South African Art,
Human & Rousseau, Cape Town

Walton, James

*Homesteads and Villages of
South Africa,*
J. L. van Schaik, Pretoria

Willcox, A. R.

The Rock Art of South Africa,
Thomas Nelson and Sons (Africa),
Johannesburg

Wolpowitz, Lily

*James and Kate Hyde and the
Development of Music in Johannesburg
up to the First World War,*
J. L. van Schaik, Pretoria